D1602295

Social Work and Genetics:
A Guide for Practice

Social Work
and Genetics:
A Guide for Practice

Sylvia Schild
California State University, Sacramento

Rita Beck Black
Columbia University

The Haworth Press
New York • London

Social Work and Genetics: A Guide for Practice is monographic supplement #1 to the journal *Social Work in Health Care*, Volume 9, 1984. It is not supplied as part of the subscription to the journal, but is available from the publisher at an additional charge.

Social Work in Health Care is a quarterly journal of medical and psychiatric social work.

The Haworth Press, Inc., 10 Alice Street, Binghamton, NY 13904–1580
EUROSPAN/Haworth, 3 Henrietta Street, London WC2E 8LU England

Library of Congress Cataloging in Publication Data

Schild, Sylvia, 1919-1983.
   Social work and genetics.

   "Monographic supplement to the journal *Social Work in Health Care*, Volume 9 (1984)" – CIP t.p. verso.
   Bibliography: p.
   1. Genetic counseling. 2. Medical social work.
I. Black, Rita Beck. II. Title: Social work in health care. III. Title. [DNLM: 1. Social work. 2. Hereditary diseases. 3. Genetic counseling. W1 S0135p v.9 Suppl. / QZ 50 S334s]
RB155.S285   1984   362.1'96042   84-560
ISBN 0-86656-193-5

CONTENTS

List of Figures

List of Tables

Foreword

FROM A SOCIAL WORKER

Readers of this remarkable volume have both a zestful and a sobering experience ahead. The late Professor Sylvia Schild and Professor Rita Beck Black, their guides, have been among the foremost social work practitioners/theorists/educators in the relatively new field of genetic counseling. I say relatively new because social workers began practicing in this specialized area only two decades ago compared to the almost eight decades of the profession's experience in general medical social work.

The progress in genetic knowledge over the last 20 years, current developments in genetic screening and in prenatal diagnosis, and anticipated developments in gene therapy make this rapidly growing biomedical field an area of exceptional growth potential for social work. But despite the increase in genetic knowledge and technology, understanding of the psychosocial implications of genetic disorders for afflicted, nonafflicted, and carrier members of the family has been slow to develop and to be appreciated. Thus genetic counselors, including social workers, are in short supply compared to the rapidly growing numbers of individuals, couples, and families now seeking information, screening, and counseling.

Out of their combined years of rich clinical and research experience in genetic counseling and other health care practice, Professors Schild and Black set the stage herein for the fulfillment of social work's potentialities in this area of practice. Their analysis is soundly embedded in a valuable historical perspective on the development of genetics from its origins, including the eugenics movement of the late 19th and early 20th centuries, and on the development of social work's participation in genetic counseling. With admirable clarity, they conceptualize the biopsychosocial perspective of social work, its "fit" with the health care field in general, and with genetic counseling in particular. They delineate a fine balance between what genetic counseling holds in common with other forms of health care social work, and what is unique about it for the social worker. The uniqueness lies largely in the meaning of genetic disease to the individual derived from the fact that every cell in one's body carries the defect. The disease cannot be separated from any part of one's body. This fact may lead to a sense of spoiled identity, intensified by varying degrees of risk for transmitting the defect to one's children, and by guilt and grief with the unanticipated birth of a defective child. In turn, social work is uniquely qualified to help those facing these and other psychosocial issues in genetic disease.

With profound empathy, the authors describe the ethical and value dilemmas for the family and for the social worker seeking to help clients make reproductive decisions concerning abortion vs. carrying a fetus to term, child-bearing vs. adoption or childlessness or new forms of reproduction, on the basis of noncertain, probabilistic information—and often with little or no time for due deliberation. The ethics of informed consent, of genetic screening, and of decision making are explored with deep respect for the complexities involved. The insights developed can be generalized to value and ethical dilemmas in all social work practice in health care. This alone is a significant contribution, for new and presently unanticipated dilemmas are generated continuously as biomedical technology advances. A framework is presented for understanding the components of decision-making and risk-taking behaviors in issues having no clear resolution.

The authors explain complex forms of inheritance clearly, but not simplistically, and a helpful glossary is also provided. Case examples illustrate technical and professional concerns, and underscore the connections between the psychosocial needs of afflicted families and the knowledge, values, and skills of social work. It is clear that as developments in this biomedical field continue, all health care social workers will benefit from this landmark contribution to the social work literature. But the benefits are not limited to health care social workers. The authors suggest direct applicability to other fields of practice such as child welfare. For all social workers serving families and individuals in *any* field, I believe the knowledge, perspective, and skills conveyed in this volume will be important professional equipment in prevention, intervention, education, and referral as they help clients who face problems and decisions raised by developments in genetics. The same may be said for those engaged in research, planning, program development, and policy advocacy.

Few social workers have the opportunity in their professional careers to discover, explore, occupy, and begin the settlement of a new area of practice for their colleagues. The late Professor Schild and Professor Black have made productive and exciting use of their distinctive opportunity, thereby benefitting their own profession as well as other disciplines involved in genetic counseling.

Carel B. Germain
The University of Connecticut
Graduate School of Social Work

FROM A GENETICIST

Genetics has been reborn—yet again. The past two decades have seen a meteoric rise of genetics as a science and as a clinical discipline. One is reminded of two earlier periods of excitement. At the turn of the century, Gregor Mendel's fundamental laws of genetics had to be rediscovered before being circulated widely through the halls of science. Two decades later, the eugenics movement caught the fancy of social engineers, only to find itself used to support blemished laws and faulty public policy.

Today, again, there is an urgency about genetics, an insistence for a place in the public consciousness and in public policy. We find the subject being discussed by educators, by legislators, by commissions concerned with public safety or grappling with new problems in bioethics, and, finally, by individuals confused about the impact of genetics on their own health and on basic concepts about themselves. Knowledge and understanding about genetics are still limited. Too often the field is encompassed by mythology, by a sense of mystery and awe, or by a sense of hope or a sense of fear.

The late Dr. Schild and Dr. Black recognize these complexities and the pressing need for education. Combining their knowledge of genetics with their extensive experience in social work, they have created an admirable text that translates the realities of genetics to the benefit of client and patient. Their emphasis, properly, is upon helping the individual and the individual's family. This is the tradition of social work; other institutions can and will carry other agendas.

Genetic medicine, indeed, holds high promise today, a promise of being able to control and manipulate the realities of a person's heredity as well as those of his or her environment. But the promise is not yet fulfilled in many instances. Unfortunately, preknowledge of untreatable disease, altered life plans, and deep disappointments and personal tragedies often surround genetic diagnoses even though successful therapies and attractive choices are increasingly available. Social workers must traverse many complex issues with their clients; they will have to interpret genetic facts for them, and help them find ways to cope with those facts and deal with the available choices. This book is meant to provide the necessary information and guidance to social workers facing those tasks. It should prove to be a most useful resource.

Maurice J. Mahoney, MD
Professor, Human Genetics
Pediatrics and Obstetrics/Gynecology
Yale University School of Medicine
New Haven, CT

Dedication

Sylvia Schild, DSW
6/19/19 – 9/19/83

It was with shock and sorrow that I learned of Sylvia Schild's unexpected death just shortly after we completed work on the manuscript for this text. Dr. Schild's contributions to the field of social work extend over her long and fruitful professional career. Her early writings on social work and families of the mentally retarded continue as basic references. Her recent publication on the ongoing needs of these families after diagnosis testified to her continued interest in that topic. The publication in 1966 of Dr. Schild's article, "The Challenging Opportunity for Social Workers in Genetics," marked the beginning of the profession's recognition of the important contributions that social work could make to the then relatively new field of genetic services. Tremendous growth in both genetics and social work's involvement followed in the intervening years, and the present volume proudly documents the rich contributions that Dr. Schild and a growing number of other social workers have made to the genetics field in the less than 20 years that have passed since that early article.

My own work with Sylvia began in 1974 when I approached her as a new graduate student eager to become involved in the exciting arena of social work and genetics that she had described in her writings. Over the years, as we moved from being teacher and student to becoming mutual colleagues and friends, Sylvia shared with me both her warm generosity and unfailing enthusiasm for social work. I am grateful not only that we were able to complete this volume, which expresses so much of what Sylvia believed, but also that so many others are now continuing the work in the field of social work and genetics that she loved so much.

RBB

Preface

The idea for a book on social work and genetics grew out of our long-held interest in the impact of genetic disorders and services on the lives of people. Our clinical experiences in genetic counseling fostered our strong conviction that social work has much to contribute in the provision of genetic services. The many breakthroughs in genetic knowledge and technology carry significant import for clients; for medical diagnosis and treatment; and for family planning, marriage, family relationships, and personal functioning. Clients with genetic concerns and key policy and programmatic issues germane to the new genetics are encountered in most settings in which social workers practice. It is important therefore for social workers to become informed about genetic principles and services. However, only a handful of schools of social work include some content on genetics in their curricula. We thus concluded that there was a need for a book that could serve as a guide for practice for both social work students as well as practicing social workers.

Although the text emphasizes issues of clinical practice, we believe it will provide the social work administrator, program developer, or researcher a useful introduction to this field of practice. Members of other disciplines such as medicine, nursing, psychology, and education also should find useful the core content on the history of genetic counseling, basic genetic principles, social and psychological dimensions of genetic disorders, policy issues in genetic screening, and ethical and legal issues. In addition, we hope that the delineation of social work responsibilities in genetic services will assist not only in the expansion of social work's involvement but also in enhancing interdisciplinary collaboration in genetic programs.

We wish to express our gratitude to the following social work colleagues who generously shared with us case illustrations from their practice: Joan Burns, Dolores Conroy, Judy Goldring, Judith F. Harold, Diane Plumridge, Janis Spurlock, and Joan Weiss. The contributors' names have not been attached to their specific reports, as an additional measure to safeguard the privacy of their clients, all of whose identities have already been appropriately disguised. Their case materials, plus those we have drawn from our own practice experiences, add a vivid reality to discussion of the nature of life problems affecting genetic clients and the contributions of social work in this new service arena.

xvi SOCIAL WORK AND GENETICS

We are particularly indebted to Sylvia Clarke, Editor of *Social Work in Health Care,* for her most helpful comments and suggestions, and to Maurice J. Mahoney, MD, for his careful review of the manuscript for scientific accuracy.

Sylvia Schild
Rita Beck Black

Social Work and Genetics:
A Guide for Practice

1

The Case for Social Work in Genetics

Genetic counseling, in my concept at least, is a type of social work entirely for the benefit of the whole family without direct concern for its effect upon the state or politics. (Reed, 1974, p. 336)

In many ways, genetic counseling has a greater kinship with health and clinical psychology, psychiatry, social work and mental health than with biology and genetics out of which the field originally developed. (Kessler, 1979, p. 4)

THE BIOPSYCHOSOCIAL PERSPECTIVE

What is the social work-genetics connection? A valid question, for on the face of it these appear to be two very disparate fields. The relevance of social work to genetics is understood best in the context of the knowledge base required for effective social work practice. Ewalt (1980) identifies that:

the boundary of clinical social work practice and the particular role of clinical social work within the mission of the social work profession is thought to be represented by the ability to conduct a biopsychosocial assessment of person-in-situation and to conduct or facilitate interventions based on these assessments. (p. 23)

The current definition for clinical social work that has been proposed by the National Association of Social Workers contains two important premises pertinent to the social work-genetics connection. First is the concept that the individual as a biological, psychological, and social being is indivisible. And, second, that a dysfunction in any of these elements disturbs equilibrium and creates or aggravates tensions in both the individuals and those close to them. Furthermore, it is emphasized that inquiry into the state of health is a requirement in any form of clinical practice. "Sensitivity to the interactive effect of biological function on the

1

behavior or the condition under investigation is always necessary and sometimes critical'' (Cohen, 1980, p. 27).

From this perspective, all social workers clearly need, as a part of their professional knowledge base, basic information on genetics and the impact that genetic disorders can have on the lives of people. The social worker employed in a specific genetic service may require more in-depth understanding of human genetics and clinical procedures in order to carry out specialized tasks required by the genetic setting. However, since the psychosocial functioning of an individual at any given moment is greatly influenced by his/her genetic endowment and by the state of health, physical fitness, and appearance (Regensburg, 1978), social workers in all settings need to be sensitive to and knowledgeable about genetic differences in people, the meanings given to those differences, and their resulting effects on behavior. Northen (1982) has pinpointed several areas of psychosocial functioning subject to the influence of genetic endowment: (1) capacity to achieve a positive state of health; (2) constitutional strengths or weaknesses that influence the course of the individual's development; (3) physical activity and appearance; (4) expectations held by others for one; and (5) self-esteem and identity. Northen states:

> Illness and physical defects that are in one's heredity or to which a person is predisposed not only threaten life and health, but also tend to carry feelings of inferiority, stigma, anger at parents and other ancestors, guilt, and the fear concerning transmission of a defect to others. (1982, p. 38)

The potential stresses and disruptions in functioning resulting from genetic diagnoses cover familiar ground for social workers. These psychosocial problems fall well within the profession's concern for individuals in their interpersonal relationships and environmental encounters. Thus, the content of this book is germane to the range of social work practice: in clinical work with individuals, families, and groups; and in policy, planning, and administrative work directed to the development of genetic and social service programs that are sensitive and responsive to the needs and concerns of genetically affected clients and their families.

Relationship to the Health Field

From its beginnings as a profession, social work has demonstrated a strong commitment to serving individuals and families whose health problems have influenced their psychosocial functioning in significant ways. The emergence of medical social work at the turn of the twentieth century as the first professional specialization attests to this concern, as does the contemporaneous involvement of social work at all levels of health care (Bracht, 1978). Both social work education and literature currently reflect the heightened activity in the health field. This upsurge of activity by the social work profession has coincided with growing societal considerations about health care delivery, environmental hazards, and quality of life issues for the disadvantaged and handicapped members of the general population. Concomitantly, the burst of scientific discoveries in knowledge and technology has presented fresh hopes and possibilities for better treatment, and in some cases, the promise of cure and prevention. Nowhere is this more evident than in the field of genetics. New advances have led rapidly to the evolution of the medical specialty of clinical or applied human genetics and its accompanying service of genetic counseling. Connections between human genetics with the field of public health also have grown as genetics programs have increased their efforts to prevent genetic disorders through prenatal diagnosis, counseling about reproductive risks, and screening for carriers of genetic diseases.

Social workers located in medical and public health settings have led the way for the profession in identifying and addressing the needs of clients with genetic concerns. This involvement can be expected to increase as genetic knowledge and services continue to expand. As the data provided in the next section confirm, there are a significant number of genetically affected individuals, who, along with their families, can benefit from professional social work service.

The Population to Be Served

Everyone is at some risk for experiencing the impact of genetic disease, since each individual is endowed with four to eight deleterious or altered genes. The normal development and functioning of every person depend on genetic information transmitted by both parents and expressed in interactions with environmental factors. "Rare is the family that is entirely free of genetic disorder—however mild or insignificant—of genetic predilection or of genetic-environmental effects" (Milunsky, 1975, p. 1). Although closely associated with birth defects, genetic diseases are found in all age groups and have great variability in their expression. Disorders with genetic components such as mental retardation, congenital malformations, cancer diseases in families, diabetes mellitus, hypertension, schizophrenia, and skin and allergic diseases are conditions familiar to most people. Some defects have ethnic or racial predilections that place certain population groups at risk. A few statistics on genetic disease dramatize the enormous magnitude of the problem:

— 12 million Americans carry true genetic disease due wholly or

partly to defective genes or chromosomes — 35 percent of all spontaneous abortions are caused by gross chromosomal defects
(amounting to more than 100,000 per year in the United
States) — 40 percent or more of all infant mortality results from
genetic factors — 4.8 to 5 percent of all live births have genetic defects — 4/5ths (approximately) of the mentally retarded are believed to carry a genetic component to their disability — 1/3 (approximately) of all patients admitted to hospital pediatric wards are
there for genetic reasons — Each of us carries between 4-8
recessive genes for serious genetic defects, and, hence, stands a
statistical chance of passing on a serious or lethal condition to each
child. (U.S. DHEW, 1975)

Estimates of the number of potential clients with genetic disorders can
be derived from a variety of sources. For example, reports indicate that
approximately 150,000 to 200,000 babies born each year will be diagnosed as having a birth defect, i.e., a structural or metabolic disorder that
is genetically determined or is caused by environmental influences occurring during embryonic or fetal development (Sorenson, Swazey, &
Scotch, 1981). When it is recognized that each of these children is born
into a family, it is readily apparent that there are probably as many as
one-half to three-quarters of a million people involved each year in the
families of these children:

It is from these families, with their plans, expectations and hopes for
the future that genetic counseling clients come . . . . they bring
with them not only questions about why and how birth defects happen, but questions about what can be done, concerns about how to
care for the affected child, and also questions about their families,
its resources and relationships within the family. (Sorenson et al.,
1981, p. 131)

A second estimate of the size of the potential client population can be
developed by extrapolating from a study that estimated the need for
genetic services in California (Epstein, Erickson, Hall, & Golbus, 1975).
Their data provide a basis for a rough estimate of the national need, since
California has about 10% of the total population in the United States. This
study estimated that a combined annual caseload for genetic services of
17,000 annually existed for California alone, based on only a 50% utilization rate and excluding any estimates of screening programs for carrier
status. Multiplying even this conservative figure by a tenfold increase for
a national estimate yields a population of considerable magnitude.

It is entirely reasonable to believe that social workers as a group see
more people with genetic problems than are at this time seen in genetic

clinics. For example, as recently as 1973, it was estimated that about 98% of the people who could benefit from counseling about genetic problems were not seen by genetic counselors (Sly, 1973). Social workers meet a great number of clients with genetic problems in medical settings such as facilities for the care of high risk infants and pediatric, neurological, endocrine, or other specialty clinics. Other settings that also yield a large share of clients with problems having genetic implications include family planning services, adoption and child welfare agencies, family service agencies, child guidance clinics, public health programs, agencies serving the mentally retarded and their families, and even welfare departments that now serve many developmentally and physically disabled clients.

NEW DILEMMAS AND UNANSWERED QUESTIONS

The current boom in genetic activities has generated considerable excitement for scientists and lay people alike. Gene splicing, test-tube babies, prenatal diagnosis, and fetal surgery tantalize the imagination of most everyone. These dramatic advances offer new hope but at the same time raise many perplexing dilemmas for which precedents and guideposts for decision making and action are absent. The controversial moral and ethical issues raised by the tampering with natural processes have become politicized as well, as seen in the current lobbies for and against abortion. The complex issues engendered by the new genetic advances have had an influence on public policies and attitudes governing such endeavors as research with human subjects, medical services based on new technologies such as artificial insemination and in vitro fertilization, and commercial enterprises based on recombinant gene knowledge and methodology. There are no simple, easy answers to the complex issues that arise and are confronted daily. As increasing numbers of clients seek genetic services, more and more troubling questions are being asked. For example, the complexities in prenatal diagnosis are just beginning to be identified. If a pregnant woman learns through an ultrasound examination that the fetus she is carrying has a cleft lip, does she have the right to the legal abortion she requests on the basis of this cosmetic defect? Should there be any limits on elective abortions? Whose value judgments should be given priority?

It has become apparent that some of the concerns for which genetic clients seek help introduce ethical considerations that impinge on the nature of the social work practice itself (Lowenberg & Dolgoff, 1982). Complex legal dilemmas also frequently are bound up in these areas of ethical concern. In the example cited, the social worker will want to help the pregnant woman think through all the implications before reaching an informed decision. Should the worker support the client's desire for abortion? Is this not congruent with the professional value and practice principle of fostering the client's right to self-determination? Should the rights and interests of the yet unborn child play a part in the decision? Are such rights more a matter of ethical or legal concern? If the physicians resist abortion, believing the cosmetic defect constitutes insufficient grounds for the procedure, will the social worker press this view on the client? What are the legal rights of the mother to utilize the available technology as she wishes? For whom, mother or fetus, will the social worker advocate? What is the ethical decision here? What are the legal requirements? Lacking precedents to follow, each novel situation in clinical genetics is apt to pose important, sometimes torturous, questions for resolution by all parties concerned: professional service providers, clients, and significant family and friends, as well as legal and legislative officials.

The highly publicized genetic advances, although enmeshed in controversy, spur new hopes for afflicted individuals and their families, and stimulate increasing numbers to seek out genetic services and counseling. Although the promise of dazzling things to come through genetic engineering will not generally become pragmatic realities overnight, significant progress has been achieved in human genetics in recent years. It is now possible for genetic counselors to supply families with diagnoses, reproductive risks, and in some cases, even prenatal diagnosis for many heretofore mysterious disorders. Unfortunately, these new services, although significant and valuable, also contribute new psychological and social stresses for the recipients.

PSYCHOSOCIAL IMPLICATIONS OF GENETIC DISORDERS

There are social and psychological accompaniments of genetic disorders that may be problematic for clients and counselors. The genetic counseling service may be stressful in and of itself, as it often deals with sensitive content and with uncertainty (Black, 1979, 1980a). Even when the final outcome of the genetic counseling process yields "good" news for the family, there may have been fears and anxieties aroused during the diagnostic period before definitive results were known.

The potential impact the genetic diagnosis and disorder can have on affected persons has been noted by social work writers to impinge seriously on both affected individuals and their families (see for example, Black 1979; Kiely, Sterne, & Witkop, 1976; Plumridge, 1976; Schild, 1977a,b; Weiss, 1981). Quotations directly from parents of genetically affected children illuminate sharply some of the intense emotional reactions and anxieties which may be experienced:

I keep thinking of what I've done to my children . . . . I feel as if I have been branded and the mark is on my forehead for everyone to see (parents of children with phenylketonuria [PKU]). (Schild, 1968)

That (aberrant chromosome) didn't mean much to me . . . it still doesn't mean a lot. I think probably way down deep, I still don't believe that a tiny particle should make a difference to her . . . . While it (the chromosomal disorder) came as no surprise, I still didn't feel it for awhile. I was numb. . . . It's one of those things that you don't want to believe even when you are knowing it. It has to grow on you (mothers of children with chromosomal defects). (Plumridge, 1980)

He (husband) couldn't accept it. He had never known anything like it to happen in his family. He kept wondering ''why?'' He kept searching back, looking for a cause and asking ''why?'' . . . . I feel horrible, just horrible . . . . Why did I have something like this? I'm good (mothers of children with Down syndrome). (Kramm, 1963)

Highly charged emotions and concerns similar to those illustrated in these quotations may be experienced by the genetically affected individuals themselves. In addition, pain, confusion, and apprehension may be manifested by extended kindred and significant others. The social needs evoked by the diagnosis often require new coping strategies for successfully meeting the demands. The nature of the specific disorder and its ramifying effects on various aspects of functioning may shape individual behaviors and the social relationships of affected individuals. Thus, the genetic situation may influence relationships and interactions with other persons and institutions in the social environment.

Clients bring to genetic counseling concerns that go far beyond technical issues of diagnosis, etiology, and recurrence risks. A recent, large-scale study of genetic counseling and its effectiveness (Sorenson et al., 1981) confirmed this observation. As might be expected, the two most frequent reasons given by female clients for seeking genetic counseling were: (1) to learn more about the etiology of the medical problem (58%) and (2) to learn what risks there were for recurrence of the problem in future children (54%). Although not reported in detail, data on male clients were similar to those on females. The researchers discovered, however, that a significant minority of clients also came with a number of what were termed ''sociomedical'' as opposed to ''genetic-medical'' questions. The most frequent sociomedical concerns cited by clients were: (1) feelings about having an affected child (26%), (2) school or other special programs (20%), (3) financial costs of raising a child with a birth defect (20%), (4) their relationships with their other children (11%), and (5) their relationships with their husbands (10%). Unfortunately, in this same investigation the researchers also found that clients coming to genetics clinics had less chance of having these socio-medical concerns addressed than their genetic-medical questions.

It is clear that psychosocial concerns do exist and need to be considered when providing genetic counseling and related services to this population. The kinds of sociomedical concerns identified in the cited study fall into the domain of client problems appropriately served by the social work profession, and indeed, the value and potential for social work involvement in the area of genetic services have been identified in the fields of both social work and genetics (see, for example, Black, 1980b; Committee, 1975; McGrath & Owen, 1975; Nesser & Sudderth, 1965; Schild, 1966, 1973, 1977a,b; Tips, Smith, Lynch, & McNutt, 1964; Weiss, 1976). This growing body of literature documents the vital part social work can play in relation to the field of genetics.

ROLE FOR SOCIAL WORK

Social work practice with clients who have genetic problems and concerns can take place in any social work setting in which the genetic needs are expressed or identified as crucial to the life problems of the client (Schild, 1977a). Regardless of the setting in which the social worker practices, the objectives of working with the clients who have genetic concerns are the same. Invariably, the major goal is to help the individual and the individual's family cope with the dislocations and disturbances occurring as a result of the genetic diagnosis and/or presence of a genetic defect or disease (Schild, 1977b). The primary goal of social work in genetics is not to prevent genetic disorders. The major aim is to improve the quality of life of affected individuals in the face of any limitations or liabilities that might be imposed by the genetic problem and to influence the development of genetic services that are sensitive and responsive to the needs of genetic clients. In this sense, the goal of social work with genetic issues is but a specific extension of the purposes of all social work practice; the specialized genetic counseling process that goes on in genetics programs represents only one point in a large network of services that can rightfully be seen as part of a continuum of genetic social services.

Because of the wide-ranging ramifications of genetic disorders, the needs of clients often will not cease even after the most successful genetic counseling experience. Social work services may be in order at many levels of the transactions between genetic clients and their environments—from the direct provision of preventive counseling or crisis intervention, intake services, counseling, and supportive casework to the activities of consultation, planning, education, research, and evaluation geared to the enhancement of genetic services. A growing body of knowledge has emerged that provides a basis for social work practice in these roles. In this book we consider this content and its implications for social work practice in relation to genetic concerns and issues.

2

Historical Perspectives:
Genetic Counseling and Social Work

GENETIC COUNSELING: HISTORICAL DEVELOPMENT

While relatively new as a specialty in medical practice, genetic counseling in a nonprofessional sense is ancient. Louro (1981) writes:

> birth defects have been known, feared, and dreaded since the earliest time. In antiquity, birth defects were interpreted as messages of the gods . . . in the main, they were decoded as dreadful harbingers of doom. By 5000 B.C., there were descriptions of 62 different malformations inscribed in the records. (p. 14)

The Bible contains some references to giving advice about marriage that suggest consideration of heritability issues. There also are numerous examples of mores and customs relative to inherited disorders: for example, even up to the present day, marriage brokers in Japan are concerned with "familial" diseases. They take family pedigrees and use such information to advise for or against the marriage. All of us are aware of the social significance given to blood lines. Probably from the beginning of time, human beings have been concerned about the transmission of both positive and negative features to their offspring.

Formalized programs of genetic counseling evolved at a much later date in history and were molded by the prevailing state of genetic knowledge and the social philosophies of the day. Genetic counseling, as we know it today, reflects the rapid rise in the prominence of genetics in the past five or six decades due to outstanding advances in scientific knowledge and technologies. Yet to understand some of the current dilemmas in the field of genetic counseling, it is necessary to look back even earlier and to examine its early growth in the United States and the meteoric rise and fall of its forerunner: the human eugenics movement.

The Human Eugenics Movement

Reed (1974) credits Sir Frances Galton as paving the way for the development of genetic counseling. Galton was the first to use measures to study the contributions of heredity and environment in the development of human traits. His connection with genetic counseling relates to his involvement in eugenics, which is defined as the science that deals with the improvement of races and breeds, especially the human race, through the control of hereditary factors. Galton, in 1865, stated that "if a twentieth part of the costs and pains were spent in measure for the improvement of the human race that is spent on the improvement of the breeds of horses and cattle, what a galaxy of genius might we not create" (in Reed, 1974, p. 333). Lacking a scientific basis, the early genetics movement floundered at first, but the rediscovery in 1900 of Mendel's classic paper of 1866 marked the movement of genetics into the modern era; it brought genetics into prominence and paved the way for the undercurrents of interest in genetics to be transformed into a stable, institutionalized movement (Ludmerer, 1972). Human genetics in the early 1900s was interwoven with eugenics to the extent that nearly everyone regarded research in human genetics as "pure" eugenics. Davenport, a leader in the eugenics movement, stated in 1923 that "human heredity is the leading branch of eugenical research" (Ludmerer, 1972, p. 50). Despite a scientific foundation limited to Mendel's basic laws of inheritance, the eugenics movement advanced a two-pronged program consisting of *negative* and *positive* eugenics. Negative eugenics had the goal of preventing the reproduction of those judged as "unfit"; positive eugenics aimed to encourage the reproduction of the "fit" to promote racial betterment.

Ironically, the first third of the 20th century, when eugenics flourished, also was the period in which basic genetic research began to identify the true complexity of inheritance. Early research findings showed that a certain degree of variation was due to chance environmental factors and not genetic influences; that the elimination of a trait from a population requires an extraordinarily lengthy, complex process; and that most, if not all, traits are determined by a great many genes. The results of the Binet intelligence testing of Army inductees during World War I severely challenged prevailing beliefs in the hereditary nature of feeblemindedness. Of the 1.7 million recruits tested, "47 percent of the Caucasians and 89 percent of the Negroes were found by eugenic standards to be feebleminded" (Ludmerer, 1972, p. 78). Obviously the test was not able to discriminate the different backgrounds of those examined. The findings raised increasing suspicions about intelligence tests as accurate measures of innate or inherited intelligence, a controversy which still persists, as indicated in recent debates over the relative contribution of environment and heredity to IQ scores (see, for example, Kamin, 1974; Loehlin, Lindzey, & Spuhler, 1975).

The American eugenics movement, composed largely of nonscientists, was unresponsive to this newer genetic knowledge. The movement became intellectually static and unchanging in its leadership and failed to attract new followers, especially as it became more racist in attitude. Ironically, the movement did have some positive influence on geneticists and the field of human genetics. As eugenics misused genetic science more and more blatantly, many noted geneticists felt obligated to denounce publicly the movement, thus becoming the first group of scientists to raise the issue of what constitutes the investigator's social responsibility concerning the social application of his/her discipline. At the same time, however, the misuse of genetic science by eugenicists also brought disfavor on human genetics. Because the two fields were so closely interwoven, both eugenics and the reputation of human genetics fell into disrepute.

The Evolution of Clinical Human Genetics

How then can we explain the fact that in 1963, Fraser would write that "human genetics is having its heydey"? Despite the low point of human genetics in the 1930s, a few persistent, dedicated geneticists continued their efforts and gradually attracted a group of new workers. The field progressed steadily throughout the 1940s, but it was only after World War II that social events once again strongly influenced the growth of human genetics. The advent of the atomic bomb, with its threats of radioactivity and resultant mutations, spurred interest in genetics. Concurrently, several advances in medicine stimulated the interest of the medical profession, and physicians became more receptive to genetic science and knowledge of human genetics. First, by 1930, the emergence of bacteriology as an exact science and the beginnings of chemotherapy contributed to the rise of the average life expectancy. Doctors now began to see the more complex disorders of diabetes and heart disease, which seemed to have a hereditary background. Second, the new thrust in medicine of the importance of prevention was compatible with genetic principles. And, finally, human genetics itself began to have the tools which could be clinically applied to medical problems. Knowledge of blood groups stemmed directly from the application of population and statistical approaches to human beings, and the discovery of the "Rh Factor" (Rhesus antigen) in 1944 brought the significance of genetic data into greater prominence. The identification in the 1930s of phenylketonuria (PKU)[*1] revealed the first "inborn error" that was not exceedingly rare. This discovery took on importance in view of the fact that screening and treatment procedures quickly followed and thus made possible the prevention of the mental retardation usually associated with untreated PKU.

The years since the 1960s have been characterized by an expansion of knowledge and of services in the genetics field. Interest in the clinical application of human genetics has been sparked further by dramatic new technologies such as prenatal and newborn screening tests, and the potentials of genetic engineering and "test tube" babies. The heightened interest in genetic counseling has been reflected in increasing numbers of physicians who have chosen to practice in medical genetics and in the increasing involvement of other health professionals in the delivery of genetic services. The latter group includes psychiatrists, psychologists, nurses, social workers, and genetics associates. Lay interest in human genetics is seen in the increasing number of requests for genetic counseling and prenatal diagnosis. The dramatic growth of genetic services is illustrated by the numbers and types of programs which have evolved over the years since 1910 when the old Eugenics Office was established in New York City. By 1955, there were 13 genetic counseling clinics, 10 of these situated in academic departments of zoology and biology. Just 25 years later, there were 633 genetic service units in the United States and 142 had social services (Lynch, Fain, & Marrero, 1980). Similar programs are available throughout the world, indicating that the expansion of human genetics and its acceptance is an international phenomenon.

The 1960s and 1970s also saw the initiation and rapid expansion of active efforts to screen for various genetic diseases. Newborn screening for PKU was begun in 1963 and was followed in the early 1970s by prenatal diagnosis and carrier detection programs such as for sickle cell* and Tay-Sachs* diseases. Efforts to develop sound federal guidelines and support for such programs led eventually to the enactment in 1976 of the National Sickle Cell Anemia, Cooley's Anemia, Tay-Sachs, and Genetic Disease Act (Public Law 92-278; hereinafter, the National Genetic Disease Act). This law marked a major step forward in government support and regulation of genetic services. It provided for basic and applied research, research training, testing, counseling, and information and education programs related to genetic disease. Guidelines for insuring confidentiality and quality services also were articulated in these regulations. Under the 1981 Omnibus Reconciliation Act, genetic services have been placed under the Maternal and Child Health block grants to states, although a small amount of funding remains available at the federal level for special projects of regional and national significance. The implications of increased state autonomy in funding genetic services are not yet apparent, although considerable variability across states seems likely.

Changing Definitions of Genetic Counseling

The term "genetic counseling" was proposed in 1947 by Dr. Sheldon Reed of the Dight Institute for Human Genetics to supplant a variety of labels being bandied about, e.g., genetic hygiene, genetic advice, genetic consideration. Reed believed that genetic counseling more aptly described the service he thought of as a nondirective approach to providing genetic information and assistance without the prescriptions of eugenics. It seems likely that this effort to divorce the two concepts of eugenics and genetic counseling contributed to the rapid growth of genetic counseling. In all likelihood, genetic counseling would have been rejected if it had been presented as a technique of eugenics (Reed, 1974).

The term genetic counseling has not been free of problems, however, especially as genetic "advice giving" moved from the academic research world into the world of applied human genetics and clinical (medical) genetics. The issues of terminology and definition represent much more than mere semantic issues. Any definition of genetic counseling raises substantive questions about the basic aims and purposes of genetic counseling and who should provide such a service. As a result, definitions of genetic counseling have changed often since Reed (1974) initially coined the term and defined it as meaning "a kind of genetic social work done for the benefit of the whole family entirely without eugenic connotation" (p. 333).

Genetic counseling's eugenic roots are visible, albeit in very altered form, in its continued commitment to an overall goal of prevention of genetic disease in society. In a recent national survey of genetic counselors, over 98% rated prevention of disease or abnormality as a goal of moderate (46.5%) or high (52%) importance (Sorenson et al., 1981). In addition, a majority also attached at least moderate importance (62.5% moderate and 11% high importance) to the goal of "improvement of the general health and vigor of the population" and to "reduction in the number of carriers of genetic disorders in the population" (48% moderate and 9% high importance). However, evidence of a movement away from an exclusive orientation toward prevention also emerges from this same survey. Genetic counselors showed a strong consensus in agreeing that "helping individuals/couples adjust to and cope with their genetic problems" and "removal or lessening of guilt or anxiety" were the most important goals of genetic counseling.

Currently, the most widely accepted definition of genetic counseling, which was adopted by the American Society of Human Genetics in 1975, reflects this shift in emphasis away from a predominant focus on prevention and towards also addressing the multiple needs of the individuals involved.

Genetic counseling is a communication process which deals with the human problems associated with the occurrence or risk of recurrence of a genetic disorder in a family. This process involves an attempt by one or more appropriately trained persons to help the individual or the family to comprehend the medical facts, including the diagnosis, the probable cause of the disorder, and the available management; appreciate the way heredity contributes to the disorder and the risk of recurrence in relatives; choose the course of action which seems appropriate to them in view of their risk and their family goals, and act in accordance with those decisions; and make the best possible adjustment to the disorder in an affected family member and to the risk of recurrence of that disorder. (Fraser, 1974, pp. 636–659)

This definition implicitly acknowledges the complex interactional process that transpires between human beings, between helpers and helpees, between counselors and counselees. It identifies a movement away from the sole concern with transmitting biomedical information and toward a wider consideration of the psychological and social processes that pertain in the genetic counseling situation.

Epstein (1975) has traced his own shift from prevention to an emphasis on communication. He cites four major reasons for the change: (1) total prevention is a practical and theoretical impossibility; (2) not all persons at risk of transmitting a genetic disorder, especially a mild one, are eager to prevent its recurrence; (3) taking steps to prevent a genetic defect is in itself *not* a psychologically free process; and (4) problems present after the disorder has occurred are psychological in nature. Epstein argues that although the parental responses frequently are expressed in terms of reproductive risks, the unstated, and often much deeper concerns, center on the affected child him/herself and the ways in which they, the parents, may have produced or contributed to the child's problem. Clearly, the presence of a genetic disorder in an individual can present significant social stresses and problems in living. Parents and other family members need to master and satisfactorily resolve these issues if the goal of a healthy adaptation to the genetic situation is to be met, a stated objective in the formal definition of genetic counseling cited previously.

The acceptance of the expanded definition of genetic counseling has resulted in a flurry of writings and research to examine some of the questions it raises: How well are genetic risks being transmitted? What factors other than genetic risks influence the determination of future reproduction? Why is one risk perceived as high by some, low by others? How do individuals respond to the genetic diagnosis and to the genetic counseling process itself? What is the best approach in helping individuals to attain the "best possible adaptation" to the genetic problem? The definition reflects a growing awareness that genetic counseling is a process, taking place over time, moving in stages from the identification of the genetic disorder to the psychosocial state in which the involved individuals have learned to cope adequately with the problems evoked by the diagnosis. Counseling can be time limited and brief or ongoing and intense, depending on the severity and complexities of the genetic defect and the idiosyncratic nature of the psychosocial situation of the affected individuals.

Viewed in this light, we can see that the field of genetic counseling readily lends itself to interdisciplinary practice with the knowledge, skills and talents of several disciplines having applicability at varying points in the overall process.

As a number of writers (e.g., Griffin, Kavanagh, & Sorenson, 1976; Kessler, 1979; Sorenson et al., 1981) have pointed out, health professionals need to consider how to meet effectively the demand for genetic counseling, particularly if equal emphasis is to be placed on the words "counseling" and "genetic." Alternative means of carrying out the counseling process need to be considered, and much more knowledge is needed of the natural history of the psychosocial processes that operate when people are confronted with genetic problems. The fact remains, however, that presently most genetic services primarily are diagnostic in nature, and genetic counseling is oriented principally to the transmission of factual genetic information. The genetic centers are realistically limited in terms of finances and support staff, especially in the face of burgeoning demands for their services. These deficiencies are reflected in the results of a recent study of the effectiveness of genetic counseling. The researchers concluded that "on average, about 55 percent of the genetic-medical and only about 16 percent of the sociomedical questions and concerns clients specifically came to discuss were discussed" (Sorenson et al., 1981, p. 134). Thus it appears that despite significant progress in recognizing the complex needs of genetic counseling clients and the delicate interpersonal processes involved in genetic counseling, significant work remains if clients are to be enabled to make truly informed decisions and to cope most effectively with genetic disorders.

THE DEVELOPMENT OF SOCIAL WORK'S INVOLVEMENT IN GENETIC ISSUES

Less than 20 years have passed since the simultaneous appearance in April 1966 of Schultz' article, "The Impact of Genetic Disorders" and Schild's initial articulation of "The Challenging Opportunity for Social Workers in Genetics." These two major articles signified the opening moves in what has become an enthusiastic and energetic effort to conceptualize and develop social work practice in relation to genetic concerns.

The level of active involvement of social workers with genetic issues and their support for the development and utilization of genetic services was documented in a recent survey of social workers in health settings (Black, 1980b). At least 42% of the social workers responding to the survey indicated that they had participated in genetic counseling themselves, with many others reporting work experiences related to genetic issues. They appeared ready to become strong advocates for genetic screening and counseling services, with a high level of motivation and readiness to act in favor of genetic programs. As cited throughout this volume, the growing body of social work literature on genetic issues provides further confirmation of the profession's increasing attention to this area.[2] Highlighting these developments was the scheduling, in 1977, of a five-day institute entitled "Genetic Disorders: Social Service Interventions," sponsored by the Office for Maternal and Child Health and the Public Health Social Work Program of the University of Pittsburgh School of Public Health (Hall & Young, 1977). Its purpose was to explore both the current involvement of the social work field in genetics and the planning for future interventions. The program brought together experts in law, ethics, and medicine, as well as social work, and served as a forum for addressing a broad range of topics. Even more significantly, it served to reinforce social work's critical role in the delivery of genetic services and the importance of expanding genetic services beyond the diagnosis and transmission of medical and genetic facts (Weiss, 1980).

Along with social work's growing interest and involvement in genetic issues has come increasing recognition of the need for additional educational programs in genetics for social workers. In a survey of social work practitioners in the health field, an overwhelming majority (94%) supported greater emphasis on genetic disorders in the professional education of social workers (Black, 1980b). Another recent survey of social work leaders in health services similarly found a strong consensus that continuing education programs in genetic issues were needed by social workers (Black, 1982). Support by social work educators for the inclusion of genetics in social work education was documented as early as 1973 (McGrath & Owen, 1975). A recent repeat of that survey of schools of social work confirmed their continued support and further revealed that at least eight schools were offering special electives specifically focused on genetic issues or had offered such electives in recent years (Black, 1982).

The initial progress being made in conceptualizing the educational needs of social workers in relation to genetics was taken an important step forward when the Office for Maternal and Child Health and the Virginia Genetic Disease Program sponsored a conference in January 1980, entitled "Education in Genetics" (Forsman & Bishop, 1981). Participants at that conference focused on two related questions: (1) Which social workers need to be educated in genetics? The levels that were considered included all Master's degree students, Master's degree students in health concentrations, Master's degree students who wish a career in genetic services, and graduate social workers; and (2) What is an appropriate genetic knowledge base for social work practice at these various levels of specialization?

Recommendations were made that all social workers should have a working knowledge of genetic diseases, their etiology, and their consequences. In addition, more advanced and extensive coursework should be required of those students who specialize in health concentrations or wish to focus their careers even more specifically in the area of human genetics. The recommendations made by the conference participants reflected their concern for a comprehensive plan for incorporating genetic knowledge into all levels of classroom curricula as well as into field work training and continuing education.

It is hoped that this detailed set of recommendations will serve as an impetus for change and as a useful resource as educators and practitioners grapple with issues of curriculum revision. An exciting example of one innovative, continuing education program has been sponsored by the National Foundation March of Dimes. During the winter of 1981–82, a 26-week course on genetics was offered to social workers and nurses in the Washington, DC area. The impact of this project is currently being evaluated, and it should provide an important model for future programs.

CONCLUSION

The excitement and enthusiasm generated by the promises of genetic advances and social work's role in this challenging new arena require us to look at the controversies evident in the origins of the field of human genetics. Current dilemmas in the field can be understood better in light of its history. In particular, many questions are being raised about the scope of genetic counseling and who should provide the needed services. Indeed, there is a lack of consensus in the genetics field as to whether nonmedical or psychological matters constitute appropriate subjects within the scope of genetic counseling itself. Some clinical geneticists accept psychosocial concerns as a legitimate part of genetic counseling, whereas others circumscribe their role to deal only with medical questions and facts.

Such issues have developed out of an even more fundamental concern for the genetic client's rights to self-determination and autonomous decision making. Throughout its history, the field of genetic counseling has grappled with the inherent contradiction of its services: the goal of preventing genetic defects while at the same time preserving the right of individuals to assume the risk of bearing offspring with such defects. Because social work as a profession affirms the value of the individual's free choice, it is important that social work practice in genetic services rests on a clear understanding of these issues and their history. We are on the threshold of many potential uses of genetic knowledge that will shape life in our time. However, an alert and cautious stance is required to protect against abuses and misuses of these new advances. Present day human genetics must remain sensitive and aware of its history. A warning enunciated by Fraser (1963) remains pertinent: "let us not oversell ourselves and let us protect . . . Human Genetics from jeopardy by unqualified people speaking irresponsibly in its name. It happened before, and it could happen again" (p. 2). Social workers, along with other health professionals, have a responsibility to see that potential as well as actual misuses are not overlooked and that applications of biomedical advances such as clinical genetics are provided within the context of a carefully developed framework of helping and supportive services.

NOTES

1. Disorders marked with an asterisk (*) are described in greater detail at the end of the volume.

2. The bibliography at the end of the text provides an extensive listing of social work references on genetic issues, including a number not cited elsewhere in this volume.

3

Knowledge Base for Genetic Social Work: Basic Genetic Information

This chapter provides an introduction to the concepts of human genetics and the most frequent procedures currently used in establishing a genetic diagnosis. The first section reviews basic definitions and considers the major modes of inheritance. The second section focuses on the "genetic work-up," that is, the major reasons for seeking genetic counseling, and the types of questions, procedures, and tests that an individual or family is likely to encounter during the process of searching for a diagnosis. An overview of the procedures available for prenatal diagnosis of birth defects concludes this discussion. The goal here is not to provide a course in genetics. Rather we have attempted to provide a beginning foundation in essential principles, so that the social worker can feel comfortable in referring clients to specific genetic services, in discussing with individuals and families their concerns about genetic issues, and in identifying areas requiring further clarification or information. Genetics, as with all fields, has developed specific terminology to describe critical concepts. Throughout this chapter we will highlight those essential terms that seem to form the basic "language" of geneticists. As social workers are well aware, basic familiarity with the jargon of any field can significantly ease collaborative efforts. For the interested reader, references that provide more in-depth examination of genetic principles and specific genetic disorders are described in the notes at the end of this chapter.[1]

BASIC PRINCIPLES

A century ago Gregor Mendel proposed the notion that one generation of living species passes on its hereditary message for the continuation of the species through the transfer of "factors." Today we call those factors genes (Stine, 1977).

Genes represent the smallest unit of inheritance of a single characteristic. They are located in the nucleus of every cell and consist of various lengths of deoxyribonucleic acid (DNA). The chemical structure of each gene provides coded instructions. This code is in turn translated, after a number of steps, into a corresponding function in the cell. Genes are so small that they remain invisible even under powerful microscopes, and each nucleus contains many thousands of genes. The power of an ordinary microscope is sufficient, however, for viewing clusters of many genes which together form the larger subunits called the *chromosomes.* The place occupied by a gene on a chromosome is known as the *locus.* Chromosomes are threadlike structures which vary in size and shape and contain hundreds to thousands of genes.

Chromosomes, along with their genes, occur in pairs, with half of the chromosomes originating in the maternal egg cell (ovum) and half in the paternal sperm cell. All species of higher living organisms are characterized by their unique set of chromosomes, with the number of chromosomes remaining constant over the generations. Human beings possess 46 chromosomes in each cell, grouped in 23 identical or *homologous pairs.* The 23 chromosomes contributed by each egg and sperm cell (the *gametes*) come together in the fertilized egg to form these chromosome pairs. Each member of the corresponding pairs of genes located along the 23 pairs of chromosomes is known as an *allele.*

The chromosomes in a human cell can be viewed through a microscope, treated with a stain to increase their visibility, and photographed. After the photograph is enlarged, each chromosome in the photograph then can be cut out, arranged in order of size, and pasted on a sheet of paper to form a *karyotype.* The first 22 matched pairs of chromosomes are called the *autosomes.* The unnumbered pair, called the *sex chromosomes,* match in size only for the female where they are denoted as XX. Males have one X chromosome and a smaller chromosome called the Y chromosome. Geneticists refer to a normal karyotype as *46,XX* for females or *46,XY* for males. (Figure 1 depicts the karyotype of a male, 46,XY). New staining techniques also now make it possible to distinguish between the chromosomes based on horizontal bands revealed along every chromosome. (See Figure 1.) The patterns are consistent across all people, although very slight variations make the *banding pattern* unique for each individual. International meetings have been held to develop a numbering system that provides a universally agreed-upon set of numbers to refer to various sections of each chromosome.

Before considering the principles of human inheritance and the major types of genetic disorders, it is important to distinguish two types of cell division and the resulting differences in the behavior of chromosomes during such divisions. First of all, some sort of reduction process is necessary in order for the sperm and egg cells to unite and to form a fertilized egg that has a normal complement of 46 chromosomes, rather than twice that number. *Meiosis* is the term used for this process during which

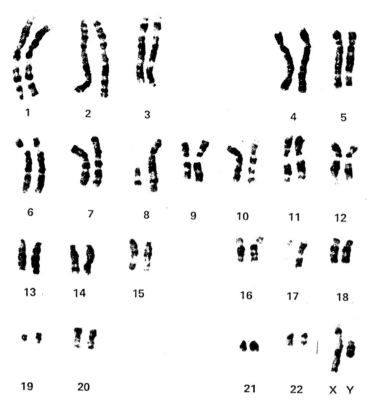

FIGURE 1. Male Karyotype. Note that the paired autosomes, chromosomes 1–22, are not recognizably different. It is the one X and the one Y chromosome that indicate this to be the karyotype of a male. Note also that the horizontal bands are the result of the staining technique utilized in the preparation of the karyotype. (Courtesy of Sanford Katz, Department of Human Genetics, Yale School of Medicine, New Haven, CT.)

the usual number of 46 chromosomes per cell is reduced to the 23 chromosomes found in egg and sperm cells. Once fertilization occurs, the process of cell division known as *mitosis* requires each chromosome to make a copy of itself and then split in half lengthwise. One copy of each chromosome then goes into a new cell for an equal division of the total genetic material. Errors that result in too many or too few chromosomes can occur in either type of division, that is, the egg or sperm can have an incorrect number of chromosomes because of an error in *meiosis,* or such an error might take place in the early *mitotic* divisions that occur after fertilization.

Chromosome Disorders[2]

Chromosome disorders involve an addition, deletion, or structural defect in a chromosome. Many specific birth defects and groups of abnormalities have been associated with chromosome abnormalities. Chromosome disorders occur in about 1 in every 200 live births with close to 20,000 infants with chromosome abnormalities born each year in the United States alone (Milunsky, 1977).

Numerical Abnormalities

Sometimes there are too many or too few chromosomes. Such abnormalities usually arise during the process of *meiosis*. This failure of the chromosome pairs to separate is known as *nondisjunction*. When the gamete (egg or sperm) with the extra chromosome joins at fertilization with a normal gamete, the resulting cell has an extra chromosome. Such a cell, with 47 chromosomes, is called a *trisomic* cell, tri meaning three, whereas a cell with 45 chromosomes would be referred to as a *monosomic* cell, mono meaning one.

The most frequent chromosome error in living individuals involves triplication of the chromosome number 21 and therefore also is called trisomy 21. This is the most common form of Down syndrome* (the other major form, which involves structural rearrangement of chromosomes, will be discussed below). Individuals with Down syndrome have 47 chromosomes in each cell of their body, with the number 21 occurring as the extra chromosome.

The problem of nondisjunction may occur with any other chromosome and usually causes severe defects in the offspring. Other early identified trisomy disorders involve chromosomes 13 or 18. Children with these disorders have multiple and severe malformations and usually do not live beyond infancy. Trisomy conditions of other autosomes are generally incompatible with life and result in early miscarriages.

The causes of nondisjunction are still unknown. Many factors, including x-ray exposure and virus infections, have been suggested, but no final answers exist at this time. It is known, however, that the incidence of nondisjunction increases with the age of the mother, rises significantly for those over the age of 35, and increases sharply after age 40. The chances at the time of amniocentesis of detecting a fetus with Down syndrome or other disorders related to maternal age are shown in Table 1. It has also been shown that once a woman gives birth to a baby with Down syndrome, regardless of her age, the chances for having another child born with Down syndrome change to a 1% risk or even higher if she is older than 35 (Carr, 1967; Hamerton, 1971; Hook & Chambers, 1977; Plumridge, 1980). It is estimated that nondisjunction occurring in the

TABLE 1

**Estimated Rates of Chromosomal Abnormalities
in Fetuses Diagnosed After Amniocentesis**

Maternal Age	Down Syndrome	All Abnormalities
29	1/850	1/750
30	1/720	1/540
31	1/620	1/370
32	1/520	1/280
33	1/420	1/220
34	1/320	1/170
35	1/250	1/140
36	1/190	1/100
37	1/150	1/80
38	1/110	1/60
39	1/90	1/50
40	1/70	1/40
41	1/50	1/30
42	1/40	1/25
43	1/30	1/20
44	1/25	1/15
45	1/20	1/12
46	1/15	1/9
47	1/12	1/7
48	1/9	1/6
49	1/7	1/4

(From Hook, Cross, & Schreinemachers, 1982)

father's sperm contributes approximately 20 to 30% of cases of trisomy 21, although data are still insufficient to prove whether there is a similar aging effect in sperm nondisjunction (Hook, 1980; Karp, 1980).

Errors of nondisjunction also can occur in sex chromosomes. The most common involve a male with two Xs resulting in a 47,XXY karyotype, or with two Ys, resulting in a 47,XYY karyotype; females may be missing an X, resulting in a 45,XO karyotype. Males with the 47,XXY karyotype are said to have Klinefelter syndrome* and commonly show tall stature, small testes and penis (often accompanied by sterility), and certain feminine characteristics (e.g., breast development and sparse facial and sexual hair that sometimes shows a feminine distribution). Intelligence may be severely impaired, although the IQ may be normal or even superior (Money, Klein, & Beck, 1979).[3,4]

Males with a 47,XYY chromosome constitution share few consistently unique features. Tall stature is very common, and other features found with increased frequency include certain skeletal abnormalities, post-pubertal facial acne, abnormal androgen levels, certain neurological findings, and reduced fertility or sterility (Money et al., 1979). Considerable controversy has arisen over the behavioral characteristics associated with the XYY karyotype because of its prevalence in prison populations. Concerns about the negative impact of labeling newborns have prevented efforts to obtain accurate estimates of prevalence in the general population, so it is impossible to say what proportion of males with this karyotype do develop behavioral problems. It should be emphasized, however, that men with the XYY karyotype have been identified who lead totally normal lives (see, for example, Noel & Revil, 1974).[3]

As noted earlier, a monosomy condition involves cells with 45 chromosomes. Only in the case of a missing sex chromosome, resulting in a 45,XO karyotype, is a monosomy condition compatible with life. Even in this instance, however, the large majority of 45,XO embryos die and are miscarried. Females who are born with this condition, called Turner syndrome,[*] are sterile; of short stature; and may have numerous health problems including orthopedic, kidney, and heart defects. "However, Turner Syndrome is the only major chromosomal abnormality so far identified that does not result in at least some degree of mental retardation" (Plumridge, 1980, p. 31).[5]

One other rare form of numerical abnormality involves *mosaicism,* a mixture of two or more different cell populations. If nondisjunction occurs during mitosis in the very early stage of embryonic development, a mixture of abnormal and normal cells throughout the body can result. The characteristics of the affected individual will depend on the percentage of normal and abnormal cells. For example, individuals who have only a portion of cells with an extra chromosome 21 may show the features of Down syndrome but in a milder form.

Structural Defects

Even when all the chromosomes are present, something may be wrong with one or more of them. These abnormalities, known as *structural defects,* occur in approximately 1 in every 500 live births (Milunsky, 1977) and result from breakage and rearrangements of one or more of the chromosomes. Breakages can occur spontaneously or result from known (e.g., viruses) or unrecognized causes. The tendency for breakage sometimes is transmitted in a family.

One form of rearrangement occurs when two small pieces break off from the ends of two different chromosomes and exchange positions. This process is called *translocation.* Translocation may occur spontaneously during meiosis (*de novo translocations*) or be inherited and passed down through a family (*familial translocations*).

When the chromosome pieces change places without any piece or portion being lost in the exchange, the translocation is called a *balanced translocation.* Unbalanced translocation is the term used when some piece or portion is lost, and it is this situation that is associated with serious birth defects. (Milunsky, 1977, p. 24)

Although individuals who carry a balanced translocation usually are completely normal in appearance and functioning, they are at risk for having offspring with deleterious, unbalanced translocations. The actual risks for giving birth to a child with an unbalanced translocation are approximately 10 to 20% if the mother carries a balanced translocation, and about 2 to 8% if the father carries the translocation. The father's lower risk suggests that abnormal sperm are less likely to survive to fertilization.

Down syndrome can also result from a translocation which yields extra material from chromosome 21. Frequently this exchange takes place between chromosomes 14 and 21 and occurs when one parent carries a balanced 14/21 translocation. When the father carries this 14/21 translocation, the chance of having a child with Down syndrome is about 2 to 5% while the risk when the mother carries the balanced translocation is about 10 to 15% (Plumridge, 1980).

Another type of structural abnormality occurs when a piece of chromosome breaks off and is lost, with no resulting rearrangement between chromosomes. This process is called *deletion.* The nature of the resulting defect will depend on which chromosome is affected and the size of the missing piece. Some deletions are more common than others, and a fairly common example is the Cri du Chat or Cat Cry syndrome in which the terminal end of the short arm of chromosome number 5 is missing. It is technically referred to as the 5p− syndrome since "p" refers to the short arm of a chromosome while "q" refers to the long arm. Children with this syndrome are severely retarded and are often recognized by their weak cat-like cry, present only in early infancy, which is due to an abnormality of the larynx.

Other structural abnormalities can occur as a result of various combinations of breaks and rearrangements. For instance, an *inversion* occurs when breaks occur in two places along a chromosome, and the segment reattaches only after turning upside down. The individual carrying an inversion may or may not suffer deleterious consequences. All of the genetic information is present in rearranged form, but gene function, to some extent at least, may depend on position within the chromosome. There is also an increased likelihood of errors occurring during the formation of gametes.

Empiric Risk Figures

Before moving to the discussion of single gene disorders, it is important to clarify one important point about the nature of the risk figures given in relation to most chromosome disorders. The types of genetic risk estimates we have discussed up to this point are known as *empiric risk figures*. They are based on data collected in epidemiological surveys and similar research projects, that is, they are derived from past experience rather than from knowledge about the specific causes of a disorder (Thompson & Thompson, 1980). Empiric risk figures also are the only currently available type of genetic estimates for the large number of disorders that result from an uncertain interaction of genetic and environmental factors (see discussion later in this chapter on multifactorial inheritance). Empiric risks stand in contrast to those risks given for single gene disorders. As indicated in the following section, single gene disorders generally follow specific inheritance patterns, each of which carries a certain risk that derives from the predictable actions of the gene involved.

Empiric data in general can provide the genetic counselor with such information as the rate of certain disorders in the population, average age of onset of a disorder, or the estimated risk of recurrence in first-degree or more distant relatives of an affected individual. Although it would be preferable to have information on the specific genetic and/or environmental mechanisms that determine the expression of a disorder, empiric risk figures can be a helpful aid in genetic counseling and decision making about reproduction. For example, the empiric risks given in Table 1 would help to clarify for a woman contemplating pregnancy the relative magnitude of the chances that she will conceive an offspring with a disorder involving an extra chromosome.

Single-Gene Disorders

Genes are usually quite stable in structure and generally can be counted on to function properly. Occasionally, however, once in thousands of times, an error is made during the replication or copying of a gene. This error, called a *mutation*, may make the gene's encoded message unreadable within the cell or may result in its being misread and mistranslated into an improperly functioning molecule. Although some mutations may by chance improve functioning or leave it unchanged, most mutations in human beings are thought to have negative consequences.

Autosomal Dominant Inheritance

As noted earlier, all genes occur in pairs along the chromosomes, and each gene in a pair is referred to as an *allele*. In *autosomal dominant inheritance* the gene product from only one allele is powerful enough to have a demonstrable effect on the individual. This may occur with harmless traits such as hair color, where dark hair is said to be dominant over light hair. When deleterious genes are dominant, however, it means that an individual with that altered gene will be affected and also will pass it on to each offspring with a probability of 1/2 or 50%. That is, each gamete (egg or sperm cell) receives either the normal or the abnormal allele of each gene pair. Figure 2 outlines the dominant inheritance pattern and illustrates the 50-50 odds that each child will be affected. It should be noted that because autosomes, rather than sex chromosomes, are involved in this pattern of inheritance, both males and females can be affected.[6]

Diagnosis of dominantly inherited disorders is often complicated by the different degrees of severity that may be manifested in individuals carrying the same altered gene. This exemplifies the distinction between one's *genotype*, which refers to the genes an individual possesses, and one's *phenotype*, which refers to the visible characteristics resulting from the expression of the genes. The diagnostic problem in many dominantly inherited disorders thus can be seen as one of great variation in phenotypes despite a common genotype. Geneticists often speak in terms of a gene being *penetrant* (i.e., has some detectable effect) and then, if it is penetrant, refer to the *variability* in its expression. One striking example is that of tuberous sclerosis.* It is a dominantly inherited disorder that can

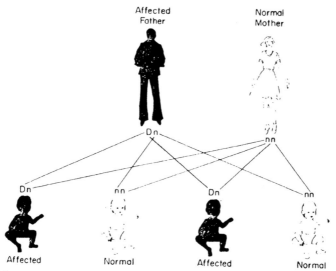

FIGURE 2. Autosomal Dominant Inheritance. One affected parent (of either sex) has a defective gene (D) that dominates its normal counterpart (n). Every child has a 50 percent chance of inheriting either the defective gene D (and then will have the disease) or the normal gene n from the affected parent. (From *Know Your Genes* by Aubrey Milunsky. Copyright © 1977 by Aubrey Milunsky, MD. Reprinted by permission of Houghton Mifflin Company.)

cause mental retardation and disfigurement in an offspring, even though the parent who carries the gene exhibits only minor skin changes.

When the minor expressions of a gene are missed (or the gene is virtually *nonpenetrant*), this variation can sometimes result in an *apparent* "skipping of generations." In actuality, no generations can be skipped because the gene must be passed from parent to child. A further diagnostic complication that can arise, however, stems from the rate of spontaneous mutations. This rate is quite high for some dominant disorders. In such cases, an autosomal dominant disorder may appear for the very first time in the offspring of totally normal parents. Very detailed clinical examinations of the parents may be required in order to rule out the possibility that one of them actually carries the gene but shows only the most subtle manifestations of it.

Another problem involved in identifying a number of dominant disorders results from their delayed onset. One such example is Huntington disease,* a progressive neurological disorder. It usually becomes manifest between 30 and 50 years of age. Individuals who know they are at risk for developing Huntington disease thus face the difficult decision of whether to forego childbearing or to have children, knowing that each child may have a 50% chance of also developing the disorder.

The most common features of this inheritance pattern are summarized in Table 2, and a listing of common autosomal dominant disorders is provided in Table 3.

Autosomal Recessive Inheritance

For many other traits, even if one of the genes is defective, the other gene is able to compensate sufficiently to allow normal functioning. In this sense, then, we speak of the mutant allele as being *recessive*. A deleterious, yet recessive, gene received from one parent will have no obvious effect on the body as long as it is paired with a normal allele from the other parent. This process enables us to remain healthy and free of unusual disorders even though we all carry four to eight deleterious genes. Once again, because the autosomes are involved, both males and females can be affected by this type of defect.[6]

The term *carrier* simply refers to an individual who is "carrying" one mutant, recessive allele that is being masked by a normal allele. *Thus we are all carriers, because we all have some defective genes.* Concern arises, however, when two individuals with the same harmful, recessive genes wish to have children. Each parent will have a 50% chance of passing his/her mutant allele to each offspring and thus a 25% chance in each pregnancy of having an affected child, i.e., one who has two mutant alleles and thus no ability to compensate for the defective genes. The details of recessive inheritance are depicted in Figure 3.

TABLE 2

Distinctive Features of the Major Modes of Inheritance

Autosomal Dominant Inheritance

1. Every affected person has affected parents and two unaffected persons don't have any affected offspring (unless there is a new mutation).
2. New mutations are important in accounting for new cases.
3. Males and females usually are affected with equal frequency.
4. Males and females can both pass on the trait to offspring (unless sterility is involved).
5. Pedigrees usually show no alternation of sexes.
6. Affected parents have a 50% risk of transmitting the gene to each offspring.
7. In general, if there is no clear pattern from one generation to the next, it is not likely to be an autosomal dominant disorder.

Autosomal Recessive Inheritance

1. It is most commonly seen in a single generation as an isolated, affected individual (i.e., often hard to distinguish from an environment cause or a new mutation), or occurs among siblings.
2. Most affected individuals will result from matings between totally healthy carrier parents.
3. Increased incidence is seen in consanguineous matings.
4. Increased incidence is seen in inbred/genetically isolated populations.

X-Linked Recessive Inheritance

1. Females are most frequently found to be carriers (heterozygotes) and ordinarily do not manifest the mutant gene.
2. Female carriers have a one in two chance of having an affected son, regardless of whether the spouse is genetically normal.
3. Pedigrees often show an *apparent* skipping of generations, i.e., alternation between carrier females and affected males.
4. New mutations are important in accounting for new cases.

Multifactorial Inheritance

1. There is an increased risk, compared to the general population, for recurrence of a disorder among first-, second-, and third-degree relatives of the affected individual.
2. For most of the more common disorders showing multifactorial inheritance, there is a baseline risk of approximately 2-5% for first-degree relatives; approximately 1/2 that risk for second-degree; 1/4 for third-degree.
3. Risk increases with increasing numbers of affected, genetic relatives, especially among first- and second-degree relatives.
4. Risk is increased if the affected person is of the sex less frequently affected.
5. Risk increases with increasing severity.

The likelihood that two individuals with the same mutant alleles will produce offspring varies with the frequency of that mutation in the population at large. Within many ethnic and racial groups certain mutations are much more frequent. Matings between related individuals, such as cousins, also will be at increased risk, because family members are

TABLE 3

Selected Listing of Genetic Disorders[1]

Autosomal Dominant (1,489 confirmed or suspected[2])

Achondroplasia	Neurofibromatosis
Huntington Disease	Osteogenesis Imperfecta (dominant form)
Marfan Syndrome	Tuberous Sclerosis

Autosomal Recessive (1,117 confirmed or suspected[2])

Cystic Fibrosis	Sickle Cell Anemia
Galactosemia	Tay-Sachs Disease
Phenylketonuria (PKU)	Thalassemias

X-Linked (205 confirmed or suspected[2])

Color Blindness	Duchenne Muscular Dystrophy
Fabry Disease	Hemophilia A and B

Multifactorial

Cleft Lip with/without Cleft Palate	Club Foot
Congenital Dislocation of the Hip	Neural Tube Defects (e.g., spina bifida)
Pyloric Stenosis	

[1]This listing provides only an arbitrary summary of some of the more "well known" genetic disorders. A comprehensive listing is available in McKusick (1983) or other texts on medical genetics.

[2]McKusick (1983).

more likely to have the same deleterious, recessive genes. It should be emphasized, however, that in *most* families the detection of a child with an autosomal recessive disorder will represent the *first* occurrence of that disorder anywhere in the extended family. (Other reasons for a negative family history are outlined in Table 4.) Tests to determine whether two parents are carriers of the same harmful gene are now available for a number of disorders and can be particularly useful in predicting risks for a few disorders that are known to occur with increased frequency in certain ethnic/racial groups. For example, Tay-Sachs disease* occurs more frequently among Ashkenazi Jews, Sickle Cell Anemia* in blacks, and thalassemia* among individuals of Mediterranean ancestry. In most cases, however, because we all carry a number of recessive genes, there is no

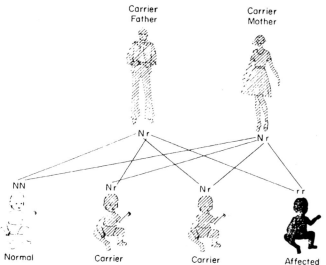

FIGURE 3. Autosomal Recessive Inheritance. Both parents are usually healthy, but each carries a defective gene that by itself generally causes no problems. Disease follows when a person receives 2 of these recessive genes. There is a 25 percent chance that a person will inherit a double dose of the defective gene; a 50 percent chance of being a carrier; and a 25 percent chance of being neither a carrier nor affected. (From *Know Your Genes* by Aubrey Milunsky. Copyright © 1977 by Aubrey Milunsky, MD. Reprinted by permission of Houghton Mifflin Company.)

TABLE 4
Summary of Reasons Why Genetic Disorders May Be Associated With Negative or Confusing Family Histories

1. There may be both *dominant and recessive forms* of the same disease. Family history and detailed diagnostic information will be needed to clarify the inheritance pattern.

2. There may be both *genetic and environmental causes*, e.g., genetic deafness vs. deafness secondary to rubella.

3. *Genetic heterogeneity.* When there is more than one genetic mechanism to account for a disorder, e.g., when two or more different, mutant genes can cause similar phenotypic problems.

4. *Lack of information* may mask the true genetic pattern; e.g., pedigrees involving illegitimacy or unknown father.

5. *Spontaneous mutation.*

6. *Late onset* expression of the phenotype. Some people in a pedigree may have died before they expressed the trait and therefore mask the genetic pattern.

7. *Variable expression.* Mild expressions may be missed.

8. *Penetrance is incomplete.* Trait is not visibly expressed; some disorders have high rates of lack of penetrance while others are virtually always penetrant.

way of predicting in advance whether two parents just happen to have the same harmful gene in common.

Common features of this inheritance pattern are summarized in Table 2, and a selected listing of autosomal recessive disorders is provided in Table 3.

X-Linked Recessive Inheritance

A different situation emerges when mutant, recessive genes are located on one of the two X chromosomes. (Thus far no harmful genes have been discovered on the Y chromosome.) When a male carries a harmful gene on his one X chromosome he has no partner allele to counteract its effects. In contrast, the female with a deleterious, recessive gene on only one X chromosome will be able to function as a healthy carrier because she has a normal partner gene on her other X chromosome.

A typical pattern of inheritance emerges (see Figure 4). Most frequently one finds an otherwise normal carrier mother who suddenly gives birth to an affected male child. She runs a 50% risk that each of her female offspring will be a carrier and each of her male offspring will be affected. Often there is an apparent skipping of generations, because carrier

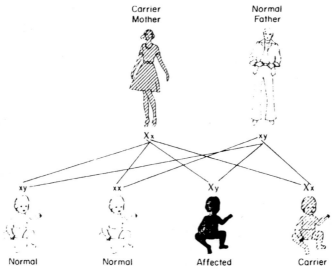

FIGURE 4. X-linked Recessive Inheritance. The defective gene is carried on one X chromosome of the mother, who is usually healthy. Disease follows when that X chromosome containing the defective gene is transmitted to a male. The odds for each male child is 50/50 for being affected, while 50 percent of the daughters will be carriers. (From *Know Your Genes* by Aubrey Milunsky. Copyright © 1977 by Aubrey Milunsky, MD. Reprinted by permission of Houghton Mifflin Company.)

females often do not show any expression of the disorder. Nevertheless, the gene, as always, will be present in every generation. Table 2 summarizes the most common features of X-linked recessive inheritance and a listing of common X-linked disorders is provided in Table 3.

Multifactorial Inheritance

A large but unknown number of defects are thought to result from a complex interaction of many genes with other genes and/or environmental factors. This form of inheritance is called *multifactorial inheritance*. It is not yet understood how environmental factors interact with genes to produce defects, but epidemiological studies clearly show a high correlation between geography, social conditions, and multifactorial genetic disorders.

Since the specific patterns of genetic transmission of multifactorial disorders are not defined as they are for single-gene defects, empiric risk figures are utilized for counseling. In general, the risks for recurrence range from 2 to 5% (among first-degree relatives) after having one affected child. The risk will be revised upward as more affected individuals are born into or are identified within a family, because that would indicate the presence of more factors placing the family at risk for recurrence. For this same reason, when the affected individual(s) have a very severe expression of the disorder, the risks may be considered to be on the higher end of the range. Both males and females may be affected by a multifactorial disorder, but for some disorders the incidence is higher in one sex, thus indicating an increased vulnerability. Thus, in those cases where an individual of the more protected sex is affected, it indicates the possibility that the family has a somewhat higher chance for recurrence.

The characteristics of multifactorial inheritance patterns are summarized in Table 2, and a listing of common multifactorial disorders is included in Table 3.

Uncertain Modes of Inheritance: The Example of Mental Illness

There are a significant number of serious disorders for which the inheritance patterns remain uncertain despite epidemiological data indicating an increased risk of occurrence among related family members. Many mental illnesses fall into this category of uncertainty. However, genetic studies of families, biological research into the fundamental causes of mental illness, and research on the effects of psychotropic drugs together are providing increasing evidence that "genetic factors are at work in many major psychiatric syndromes" (Tsuang & VanderMey, 1980, p. 1). In view of social work's significant involvement in providing mental health services to affected individuals and their families, we have included a brief review of some of the current thinking about the inheritance of mental illness. Discussion will be limited to mood disorders and schizophrenia, as these are the two major classifications of mental illness for which the most genetic research currently is available.

Estimates for the risks of occurrence of schizophrenia and mood disorders in the relatives of affected individuals are given in terms of empiric risk figures. These figures generally have been derived from three types of studies; in order of increasing precision they are: (1) family studies, (2) twin studies, and (3) adoption studies (Tsuang & Vander-Mey, 1980). Briefly, *family studies* provide general data on whether a mental disorder tends to "run in families." *Twin studies* allow researchers to compare the relative frequency of illness in identical twins (who share identical sets of genes) and fraternal twins (who share one-half of their genes in common as do all siblings). Findings that identical rather than fraternal twins more frequently share the same mental illness (or any other disorder) suggest a genetic influence, i.e., if a trait is strictly genetic, then identical twins would be expected to share that trait 100% of the time. *Adoption studies* allow researchers to begin to sort out genetic and environmental influences by compiling data on adoptees and their relative similarity to their adoptive versus biological families. Genetic mechanisms are suggested, for example, if adoptees who are separated from a biological parent with schizophrenia early in infancy continue to show an increased rate of that disorder despite no history of schizophrenia among members of their adopted family.

Convincing evidence of genetic factors in both schizophrenia and mood disorders have come from twin and adoption studies around the world. Tables 5 and 6 summarize the risks to relatives of individuals affected with schizophrenia and mood disorder. Examination of these figures suggests at least two important points: (1) although close relatives appear to be at some increased risk in comparison to the general population (10 times higher in the case of mood disorders and 10–15 times in the case of schizophrenia), the chances are higher that they will *not* develop the mental illness at all, and (2) although elevated, the genetic risks never get high enough to suggest a total genetic determination of these disorders—environmental factors clearly play large roles in both cases.

An important word of caution must be introduced, however, about the uses that can be made of these data. The figures presented in Tables 5 and 6 cannot be used as simple tools for counseling the average family in which one of these disorders has occurred. Hidden behind these summary figures are many complex issues. Recalling that empiric risk figures are used when specific etiology is not known, it must be recognized that the genetic mode of transmission has not been defined for either of these categories of mental illness. Moreover, it seems likely that a number of genetically distinct illnesses or subtypes are included under the single label of schizophrenia or mood disorder.

TABLE 5
Schizophrenia: Risks to Relatives of Affected Persons

Relation	Risk (%)	Increase Above Base Rate
First-degree relatives		
Parents	4.4	
Brothers and sisters	8.5	(10×)
neither parent schizophrenic	8.2	
one parent schizophrenic	13.8	
Fraternal twin, opposite sex	5.6	
same sex	12.0	
Identical twin	57.7	
Children	12.3	(15×)
both parents schizophrenic	36.6	
Second-degree relatives		(3×)
Uncles and aunts	2.0	
Nephews and nieces	2.2	
Grandchildren	2.8	
Half-brothers/sisters	3.2	
First cousins (third-degree relatives)	2.9	
General population	0.86	

(Adapted from Tsuang & VanderMey, 1980, p. 71)

TABLE 6
Risks of Mood Disorder in Close Relatives of Affected Persons

Patients	Ill Relatives Range of estimates (low-high)		
	Unipolar (%)	Bipolar (%)	Total (unipolar + bipolar) (%)
Unipolar	7-19	0.3-2	8-23
Bipolar	6-28	4-18	11-42

	Males (%)	Females (%)
General population	1.8	2.5

(Tsuang & VanderMey, 1980, p. 91)

In the case of schizophrenia, current data would support either an autosomal dominant mode of inheritance with reduced penetrance or multifactorial inheritance (Tsuang & VanderMey, 1980). In addition, a genetic counselor would adjust the figures in Table 5 upward or downward in relation to such critical factors as the patient's age at onset of the illness, the number of relatives affected, and the severity and type of familial cases. Although researchers believe schizophrenia includes at least several genetically distinct subtypes, the precise delineation of these subtypes has not yet been determined.

Several genetically distinct illnesses also may be included within the mood disorders. Bipolar illness (with episodes of both mania and depression) and unipolar illness (episodes of depression only) seem to be different disorders, and a genetic distinction may even exist between early and late onset forms of unipolar depression. Family studies also suggest that:

> risks are considerably higher among women than among men, among close relatives of bipolar patients than among relatives of unipolar patients. The risk to brothers and sisters of an affected person rises steeply when one or both parents also are affected. Among relatives of unipolar patients, the risk of bipolar illness appears to be very low. (Tsuang & VanderMey, 1980, pp. 96–97)

As the preceding discussion suggests, genetic counseling for psychiatric disorders can provide potentially significant information to affected individuals and their relatives, particularly in those cases where the family has assumed that the risks are much higher than research actually suggests. Careful examination of family history and confirmation of diagnosis are prerequisites for any such counseling, however, and this fact underscores the importance of referral to appropriately trained specialists for a full evaluation prior to genetic counseling. The general features of such a genetic "work-up" are considered in the next section.

THE GENETIC "WORK-UP": DIAGNOSTIC PROCEDURES AND PRENATAL DIAGNOSIS

Many individuals and families may think that they have a need for genetic evaluation, counseling, and/or prenatal testing, yet hesitate to utilize such services. Some may be uncertain whether their request legitimately falls within the domain of a genetic counseling service, whereas others may be fearful about the tests and procedures that they may be forced to undergo in order to receive genetic information. Likewise, many social workers often are uncertain about referring clients for a service of which they themselves have only a vague understanding. In this section we attempt to answer some of these questions and provide the reader with an overview of what one might expect to encounter during diagnostic evaluation or prenatal testing at a genetics clinic. Certainly each clinic will be unique in its style of operations, but the general outline should be consistent across most genetics clinics.

Appropriate Questions for a Genetics Clinic

The following questions offer an overview, from the client's perspective, of some of the main reasons people seek genetics services. They indicate that the domain of appropriate questions ranges from the most specific to the most general of concerns.

1. Do I have a genetic disorder or am I a carrier?
2. Do I have an increased risk for having one (or another) child affected with a particular genetic disease?
3. What are the implications of a genetic disease that has been diagnosed in one or both parents? What are the prognosis and treatment? Will they have an impact on plans for parenthood?
4. What help can we get in making a decision about the options of prenatal diagnosis, selective abortion, adoption, artificial insemination, etc.?
5. What kind of help is available for an already affected family member, and where can we find it? (Milunsky, 1977)

Table 7 provides a more detailed summary of the medical indications for referral to a genetics clinic.

The Diagnostic Evaluation

Even when a genetic problem is suspected and openly acknowledged by family members, there nevertheless may be some reluctance to having strangers at a genetics clinic probe into their family life and heritage. Information may be requested that has not been routinely sought in their encounters with other health professionals; apparently inexplicable measurements may be made as doctors scrutinize the bodies of parents and their children. Such experiences often increase anxiety and make it difficult for families to make full use of genetic services. Answering some of their most frequent questions about genetic evaluations can serve to reduce some of this anxiety about the unknown (Black, 1980a; Plumridge, 1980).[7]

TABLE 7

Indications for Referral to a Genetics Clinic

1. Known or presumed congenital abnormalities
   a. congenital malformations of any type
   b. ambiguous genitalia, hermaphroditism
   c. mental retardation (cause unknown)
   d. fetal or parental exposure to environmental agents (drugs; irradiation; infections; and maternal factors such as diabetes, PKU, etc.)

2. Acknowledged familial disorders
   (Knowing that a disorder is inherited is not enough information, the specific pattern of inheritance must be considered for accurate decision making.)

3. Known inherited disorders
   (To obtain information on prognosis, recurrence risks, implications for extended family)

4. Metabolic, biochemical disorders (screening)

5. Known or suspected chromosome abnormalities
   (Clarifying exact nature of abnormality becomes important because of risks for translocation carriers in extended family.)

6. Multiple miscarriages, stillbirths
   (Three or more can be used as a rough guideline.)

7. Infertility (may indicate chromosome problem in parent)

8. Premarital counseling
   (e.g., What are the baseline risks for birth defects? Do we have anything special to worry about?)

9. Consanguinity, incest

10. Prenatal diagnosis
    a. either parent is a known "balanced carrier" for a chromosome abnormality
    b. previous child with any kind of chromosome abnormality
    c. mother $\geq$ 35 years
    d. inordinate parental concern or anxiety
    e. both parents are carriers for a specifically diagnosable metabolic or structural autosomal recessive disorder
    f. either parent is affected with a specific, diagnosable metabolic or autosomal dominant disorder
    g. mother a known or presumed carrier for a serious, X-linked recessive disorder
    h. either parent has a first- or second-degree relative with a neural tube defect (e.g., spina bifida, anencephaly) or has a spina bifida defect himself/herself.

(Based on Riccardi, 1977, p. 6)

Clinical Diagnosis

A crucial component of most genetic diagnoses involves the clinical evaluation of the patient and the family. A clinical diagnosis is a determination of the nature of a disorder that is based on a careful examination of the patient and family, simple diagnostic tests that can be done with examining room equipment, and a search of medical literature for descriptions of individuals with similar symptoms or features.

The major components of a clinical evaluation include developing the family pedigree, obtaining a pregnancy and health history, obtaining a developmental assessment, and performing a careful physical evaluation (Plumridge, 1980). These steps, often accompanied by laboratory investigations which will be described below, are crucial for establishing a definitive diagnosis. *Before any genetic counseling can be provided, every attempt must be made to determine the true nature of the problem.* This is especially important because environmentally produced disorders can mimic the features of some genetic disorders. In addition, some genetic disorders with very similar features result from different patterns of inheritance that imply quite different levels of recurrence risk for a family.

Family history. The first step in the clinical evaluation is usually the taking of a detailed genetic and general medical history of the family covering at least three generations. The term *family tree* has traditionally been used to describe a diagram of family relationships, whereas the term *pedigree* is used by geneticists to emphasize the genetic focus of the information collected. The hope is that information obtained from the pedigree will provide evidence of the genetic, or nongenetic, nature of the disorder in question.

Data required for a pedigree include an accurate outline of all family and marital relationships with special attention directed to the possibility of any known common ancestors, which occurs in cousin marriages. Family members will be asked to report on any medical, physical, learning, emotional, or other health-related problems, no matter how unrelated they may seem. Such information may be critical for distinguishing between similar disorders or for revealing subtle expression of a deleterious gene in members of the extended family. Dates and causes of death of all relatives will be recorded along with a careful history of any spontaneous abortions (miscarriages) or stillbirths. This information may indicate that the disorder has occurred but gone undiagnosed in some family members. Ethnic and/or national origins also will be sought because some disorders occur with greater frequency or only rarely in certain population groups. Figure 5 shows the symbols most frequently used in drawing a pedigree, and Figure 6 gives an example of their use in a sample pedigree. Table 8 provides a brief outline of some helpful hints for systematically obtaining the information needed in a pedigree. Someone with formal training usually will be called on to construct the final pedigree used for genetic counseling. However, the social worker who constructs a preliminary pedigree with his/her client can facilitate referral to the genetics clinic by providing geneticists with basic data and alerting the client to the kinds of

PATTERNS OF TRANSMISSION OF SINGLE-GENE TRAITS

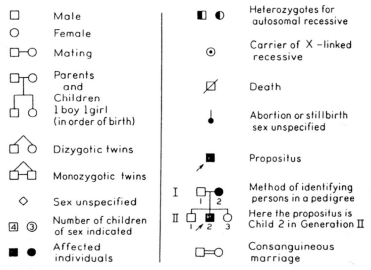

FIGURE 5. Symbols Commonly Used in Pedigree Charts. (From *Genetics in Medicine* by James S. Thompson and Margaret Thompson, 1980. Reprinted with permission of W. B. Saunders Company.)

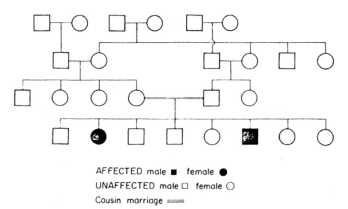

AFFECTED male ■ female ●
UNAFFECTED male □ female ○
Cousin marriage ===

FIGURE 6. Family Pedigree. This pedigree depicts autosomal recessive inheritance. Note that there were no previously affected individuals in the family; the risks for autosomal recessive disorders are increased in marriages between cousins. (From *Know Your Genes* by Aubrey Milunsky. Copyright © 1977 by Aubrey Milunsky, MD. Reprinted by permission of Houghton Mifflin Company.)

TABLE 8

Basic Guidelines for Taking Family Histories

WHO

1. Begin pedigree with the index case (identified by an arrow).
2. Include as a minimum the following living and dead relatives of the case, in this order: siblings, parents, father's siblings, all descendents of father's siblings, father's parents, mother's siblings, all descendents of mother's siblings, mother's parents, and finally all descendents of both the case and his/her siblings (i.e., work through the paternal side completely, then do the maternal side).
3. The paternal part of the pedigree arbitrarily goes on the left side of the sheet.
4. Siblings should be listed in order of birth starting with oldest on left (except for parents and grandparents).
5. Include the parents of all persons in the oldest generation shown who have the same affliction as the index case.
6. Do not include spouses of case's relatives unless relatives' offspring have some kind of disorder.
7. Include half-sibs, abortions, previous marriages, miscarriages, adopted children, and stillbirths.

WHAT

1. Inquire, as each individual is entered on the pedigree, whether or not s/he has: (a) the same affliction as the index case, and (b) any other chronic disorder or defect. Asking this for *one* individual at a time ("does he have . . . ," etc.) is often more productive than asking the question regarding a whole group at a time ("do any of these . . . ," etc.).
2. All disorders noted on the pedigree, whether the same as the index case's or not, should be described as specifically as the available information allows: e.g., qualify wherever possible the *site* and *nature* of congenital anomalies, the basis of acquired heart lesions (rheumatic, etc.), the primary site of malignancies (breast, stomach, etc.), the type of arthritis (rheumatic, gouty, etc.).
3. Check to see whether each adult is married and/or has had children *before* going on.
4. Distinguish if possible between identical and fraternal twins.
5. Enter the current age and health status of each individual under his/her symbol.
6. For deceased persons, record the age (or approximate age) at death and cause.
7. Ask routinely and note on pedigree if there is any known consanguinity among forebears. Connect husband and wife with double horizontal line if related.
8. Ask routinely for the national and ethnic origins of each family.
9. Keep in mind, when asking about the health status of each individual, that a condition may be present in some family members in a less severe form than in others (e.g., as might be suggested by a higher than usual incidence of "kidney infection" among the adult relatives of a child with obvious and severe anomalies of the urinary tract).
10. When through, ask if the disorder in question is, or was, present in more distant relatives than those mentioned. If so, identify such relatives on the pedigree.

HINT

Work in pencil on your first draft. People often remember additional details (and relatives!) only after the questioning is almost completed.

questions that the geneticists will ask. In addition, the therapeutic usefulness of genograms (Guerin & Pendagast, 1976; Hartman, 1978), a type of family tree being used by many therapists, suggests that the process of developing a pedigree with a client can serve as a vehicle for exploring many other, significant aspects of family functioning and relationships.

Pregnancy and developmental history. An accurate picture must be obtained of the developmental progress of the affected individual both before and after birth. Questions about the pregnancy will likely include the use of any drugs during pregnancy, onset and vigor of fetal activity, length of gestation, complications during delivery, birth weight and length, and any problems in the newborn period. Answers to these questions often can be useful in determining whether the disorder resulted from a genetic error expressed in early embryonic life, from an environmental insult such as intrauterine infection or *teratogen* (a substance ingested during pregnancy which causes birth defects), or from an injury during the birth process.

The developmental history considers the health and developmental milestones of the affected individual and looks especially for any delays or idiosyncratic patterns in the growth process.

Physical examination. Because a genetic error exists from the time of conception, a wide range of body systems may be affected. Some genetic disorders also result in a distinct set of symptoms that occur together; this clustering of signs and symptoms is called a *syndrome.* During the physical examination the geneticist evaluates the overall appearance of the affected individual along with any distinctive or *dysmorphic* (malformed) features in an attempt to determine whether there is in fact a pattern that fits that of a known genetic or nongenetic syndrome.

Careful measurements of many body parts will be taken and compared with established norms. Starting from the top of the head and working downward, some of the observations might include the head circumference; size and shape of the face, ears, and eyes; the formation of the torso and limbs with particular attention to any asymmetries in growth; the size, shape, and positioning of the fingers and toes; the pattern of ridges on the fingers, hands, and feet; and the pattern and amount of hair growth. Variations from established norms along any such dimensions *may* or *may not* signal a problem. Throughout the evaluation the geneticist proceeds cautiously and considers the features of other family members. For example, a distinctive nose or a strangely shaped ear may be a common family feature, unassociated with any health problems. Measurements and photographs thus may be sought of members of the extended family in an effort to determine whether certain features actually represent subtle manifestations of an underlying disorder or are only characteristic family features.

Laboratory Diagnosis

For some disorders, the clinical evaluation will complete the diagnostic work-up. There remain many genetic defects that still can be identified only by their phenotypic features, and genetic counseling in those cases must be based on the clinical evidence alone. However, chromosome analyses and laboratory tests of biochemical changes are becoming available for assisting in the diagnosis of an increasing number of disorders.

Chromosome studies will be ordered in those cases in which the clinical information suggests the possibility of some type of chromosomal defect, i.e., an error in the number or structure of the chromosomes. A small sample of blood usually is taken (1 to 5 cc, with 5 cc equal to 1 teaspoon) from the arm, or, in the case of a small child, from any large and easily obtainable vein. (Occasionally a tiny skin sample will be used as the basis for studies.) This blood sample will be processed in a *cytogenetics* laboratory. (Cytogenetics is the branch of genetics devoted to the study of chromosomes.) A delicate series of steps, usually requiring 2 to 4 weeks, will yield the final results in the form of a karyotype depicting the number and structural formation of the chromosomes.

Many single-gene disorders, especially recessive disorders, manifest themselves through an alteration in the amount or performance of crucial enzymes or other biochemicals. For example, recalling our earlier discussion of recessive inheritance patterns, it follows logically that an affected individual, who has both genes in a pair altered, often shows very low or no activity for the enzyme controlled by those genes. Such a deficiency can be looked for in a laboratory analysis. Likewise, the carrier parents who have only one altered gene for that enzyme will be expected to show a level of enzyme activity intermediate between affected and totally normal individuals. For example, Tay-Sachs disease,* a degenerative and fatal neurological disorder, is diagnosed by a blood analysis that measures the activity of an enzyme called hexosaminidase-A. Affected infants are deficient in this chemical, whereas phenotypically normal parents have half the normal amount of activity.

Other recessive disorders are marked by the production of an abnormal gene product. For example, the mutation resulting in sickle cell anemia* causes the formation of an altered type of hemoglobin. Tests on carriers reveal the presence of both normal and abnormal hemoglobin, produced by the pair of normal and altered genes respectively. Individuals with sickle cell disease will show only the altered form of hemoglobin.

Testing of potential carriers within a family can provide extremely important information for persons considering future pregnancies. Similarly, public health screening programs for carriers become possible when there is an inexpensive and easily administered carrier test for a specific disorder that is known to occur with increased frequency in a certain racial or ethnic group.

Prenatal Diagnosis

Procedures are now available for detection during pregnancy of a large number of disorders. At the present time, *intrauterine diagnosis* is the main form of prenatal testing available in the United States. The most common form of intrauterine diagnosis involves a procedure known as *amniocentesis,* a term that derives from the Greek *amnion* (the fetal membrane) and *kentesis* (a pricking or puncture). Amniocentesis involves the insertion of a needle into the membranous sac surrounding the fetus and the withdrawal of some of the fluid in which the fetus is suspended (Fuchs, 1980). Amniotic fluid is ideally sampled between 15 and 17 weeks of pregnancy when there is sufficient fluid to safely allow removal of a small portion. Suspended in the fluid are fetal cells that slough off from the fetal skin and other fetal membranes or that derive from fetal urine and respiratory tract secretions. These cells can be grown and processed in the laboratory for chromosome or biochemical studies.

The risk of amniocentesis is essentially an increased risk of miscarriage. Data from established clinics indicate a miscarriage risk of less than 1%. Such a risk augments the natural risk of miscarriage that is estimated to be 1 to 2% at this stage of pregnancy (Fuchs, 1980).

Intrauterine testing may be utilized not only for the diagnosis of chromosome disorders but also for the diagnosis of single-gene disorders for which biochemical tests have been developed. Another use of prenatal chromosome studies involves sex-linked disorders. Because the sex of the fetus is also determined with a karyotype, this procedure sometimes is used to determine whether the fetus is a male. In situations where all male fetuses run a 50% risk of being affected, some families elect abortion of any male offspring.

An important component of intrauterine testing involves the use of *sonography* or *ultrasound.* In this technique, sound vibrations are reflected off tissues of different densities. These reflections yield an image that can be used to measure the size and shape of various fetal structures (Fuchs, 1980). Ultrasound before amniocentesis allows the physician to determine the location of the fetus and placenta as well as check for twins. Sonography, in the hands of very skilled and specialized physicians, also is being used with increasing frequency and accuracy for the prenatal diagnosis of major structural abnormalities in the fetus. In addition, in a few centers around the country, *fetoscopy* is now available for certain high-risk pregnancies. This procedure allows the physician to actually view the fetus through a small, specialized device. Some visible malformations may be identified in this manner, and small samplings of fetal blood or fetal skin obtained for certain tests.

An important, recent scientific development is the ability to prenatally diagnose certain hemoglobin disorders (hemoglobinopathies) such as sickle cell anemia* and certain of the thalassemias* (Boehm, Stylianos, Antonarakis, Phillips, Stetten, & Kazazian, 1983). Since 1975, prenatal diagnosis for sickle cell anemia had been available in some cases but required the use of fetoscopy (described previously), a procedure that carries a higher risk of fetal loss than standard procedures for amniocentesis. Newer techniques utilize enzymes that divide nuclear DNA at certain points that can be consistently associated with either normal or altered hemoglobin. Fetal cells obtained through routine amniocentesis can be utilized for the testing. In addition, this technique holds exciting possibilities for future prenatal testing of other genetic disorders in which the basic defect cannot be directly detected.

In a second, recent advance, the discovery that the incidence of certain fetal malformations is correlated with elevated levels of the protein called *alpha-fetoprotein* (AFP) both in the amniotic fluid and the mother's blood has opened the way for prenatal diagnosis of yet another group of disorders (Fuchs, 1980). Most commonly these are *neural tube defects* (*spina bifida* or open spine and *anencephaly,* partial or complete absence of the brain), which show a multifactorial form of inheritance. Certain other malformations involving the kidneys, gastrointestinal tract, and abdominal wall also have been associated with abnormally elevated levels of AFP in the amniotic fluid. Sonography, utilized after the detection of an elevated AFP level, often can provide further information about the nature and severity of the defect. Parents then can make a decision about whether or not to terminate the pregnancy.

Pregnant women who have previously given birth to a child with a neural tube defect or who have a family member from either prospective parent with such a defect should be informed of the availability of prenatal testing of the AFP level in their amniotic fluid. Procedures also are now available for measuring AFP levels in maternal blood that show a similar rise with some neural tube defects. Such noninvasive testing offers the potential for wide-scale screening of all pregnant women regardless of family history. Maternal AFP screening programs currently are underway in Britain and several other European countries. Controversies in the United States over possibilities of misinterpreting results have delayed the large-scale implementation of such programs in this country (Fuchs, 1980, Kolata, 1980), although a number of states are now beginning pilot programs to provide this service to all pregnant women.

The newest advance in prenatal diagnosis is the attempt to move most of the amniocentesis-based diagnoses from the second trimester back into the first trimester. A procedure known as *chorionic villous biopsy* obtains a small sample of the *chorionic villi** that surround the embryo at 8 to 11 weeks of pregnancy. This tissue can be used for chromosome, biochemical, and DNA analyses and thereby establish prenatal diagnoses. AFP-based diagnoses could not be made, however. The biopsy is obtained with a suction catheter inserted through the vagina and cervix and advanced to the site of the chorion using ultrasound guidance. Early experience suggests that risks to the embryo are not high, but a true assessment of these risks is just now being undertaken (Simoni, Brambati, Danesino, Rossella, Terzoli, Ferrari, & Fraccaro, 1983).

NOTES

1. Milunsky (1977) provides a clear review for the reader with little or no scientific background. Riccardi (1977) and Thompson and Thompson (1980) provide excellent coverage of the major topics and disorders covered in clinical genetics; they are, however, written for the reader with at least some prior background in medical or genetic terminology. Additional references are described in Notes 2 and 3. Of particular interest are the publications by Plumridge, a social worker, described in Notes 2, 4, 5, and 7.

2. Plumridge (1980) provides an excellent discussion of chromosome disorders. It is written for use by both professionals and parents and includes coverage of the prognosis of various chromosome defects, available services, and many other specific concerns frequently raised by families.

3. For an excellent discussion of sex chromosomal disorders and their personal impact on individuals, see Money, Klein, and Beck (1979).

4. Another excellent publication on Klinefelter's syndrome is *Klinefelter's Syndrome. The X-tra Special Boy* (Plumridge, Barkost, & LaFranchi, 1982). It is written for both parents and professionals. An accompanying booklet, *For Boys Only*, is written specifically for affected boys and answers many of their frequent questions.

5. *Good Things Come in Small Packages. The Whys and Hows of Turner's Syndrome* (Plumridge, 1976) is an excellent resource, intended for use by both lay and professional audiences.

6. An exception to this general principle occurs in the case of a *sex-limited* trait, which is expressed in only one sex even though the gene determining the trait is located on an autosome. An example is one type of precocious puberty, in which heterozygous males (carriers of one altered gene) develop secondary sexual characteristics and undergo an adolescent growth spurt at about four years of age, sometimes even younger. Heterozygous females show no expression. Although affected boys are much taller at first, they soon stop growing and end up as short men (Thompson & Thompson, 1980).

7. Much of the discussion about the diagnostic evaluation has been developed from Plumridge (1980).

4

Social and Psychological Issues

A personal consciousness of difference contributes to loneliness as palpably as do physical barriers. (Featherstone, 1980, p. 54)

Mrs. L. speaks: "Everytime I see my girls suffering I feel guilty. There isn't a day that goes by when I wish I had never had children." She herself is no longer able to work as a result of the crippling effects of the same degenerative genetic disorder (trichorhinophalangeal syndrome*) that has been transmitted to two of her four children and as a single parent she has been forced to become dependent on welfare for survival.

The recent diagnosis of a genetic etiology for the family's "rheumatism" and crippling of joints has had both positive and negative effects. The family felt vindicated. School personnel for many years had accused the two affected girls, Sara, age 18, and Jane, 16, of malingering; now there was a definite excuse for the extreme fatigue, headaches, and general lassitude that had led to their frequent absences. The degenerative aspect of this rare disease was a dismal prospect, however. Jane, the most severely affected, had had a recent hip surgery and was soon to have another on her jaw. Sara, although frequently ill, had not as yet required surgical treatment; in fact, she had married three months earlier. Mrs. L. gave permission for the marriage after exacting a promise from the future husband (Tom) that the couple would not have children. Jane for the present had vowed never to marry, "I'm too sick and wouldn't be much good to anyone; anyways, I shouldn't have babies." In contrast, Laura, the eldest daughter (25 years old) appeared to be unaffected. She was married and had an apparently normal three-year-old son. Laura, however, was pregnant at the time of the genetic counseling session and elected to end the pregnancy shortly afterward. Although Laura had been told that she had not inherited the dominant disorder found in other family members, somehow she had misconstrued what she heard and believed that the genetic diagnosis explained her continuous lower back pain.

Further misunderstandings spread when Mrs. L. interpreted the genetic findings to John, her only son, 28 years of age. John also was unaffected and had one normal son from his first marriage. Since John was unable to attend the genetic counseling, Mrs. L. conveyed the results to him. She erroneously described the disorder as affecting all family members. John and his second wife thereafter began to experience marital tensions; she wished to have a child, whereas John now wished to avoid the reproductive risks which he believed were present.[1]

This case vignette vividly illustrates the complex social and psychological ramifications that can follow the diagnosis of a genetic disorder. The heightened interest in genetics and the proliferation of genetic services have led to an increased focus on the consequences of genetic diseases on the lives of people. This chapter examines the psychosocial aspects of genetic disorders in light of the growing theoretical and empirical data which are becoming available on this topic. As in any new area of research, the findings remain tentative and far from complete. Nevertheless, considerable progress has been made in identifying a number of significant factors related to the psychosocial impact of genetic concerns. These factors, which will be examined in the following sections, include: the impact of the genetic diagnosis, the common characteristics of a genetic diagnosis, the crisis issues precipitated by genetic disorders, psychological aspects of reproductive risks, the impact of amniocentesis and abortion for genetic reasons, the impact of the counseling situation, and the social service needs of genetic clients. Our review of the significant findings and views relative to these factors will provide a basis for the consideration of practice implications, which follows in Chapter 5.[2]

IMPACT OF THE GENETIC DIAGNOSIS

Kessler (1979) identifies a psychological or person-oriented approach in genetic counseling that stands in contrast to a content-oriented model that emphasizes facts and figures. The psychological approach begins with the premise that genetic counseling deals with important human concerns: health and illness, procreation, parenthood, and sometimes life and death. The psychological orientation views "the problems posed by a genetic disorder as being intimately related to the overall situation of the persons, their ways of solving problems, making decisions, and adapting to life crises" (Kessler, 1979, pp. 19-20). The shift to a psychological approach in genetic counseling reflects the growing awareness that genetic diseases evoke emotional stresses and significantly influence the life functioning of clients. A number of writers have offered hypotheses about the impact of the genetic diagnosis. Their observations raise provocative issues and deepen our understanding of the impact of genetic events.

Some authors view genetic counseling as a form of "psychologic medicine" in which consideration is given to the emotional impact of the genetic facts. Hecht and Holmes (1972) describe a complex psychodynamic counseling process which addresses stages of emotional reactions—denial, guilt, depression, and anger—through which clients must pass before they can engage in rational planning for the future. Tips and Lynch (1968) observe that "frequently intense emotional and psychological disturbances may arise within the patient and his family from implications of a hereditary etiology for the 'family disease'" (p. 110). They also describe stages of psychodynamic conflicts that almost invariably follow on the heels of a genetic diagnosis. Initial shock may lead to repression or denial of the information. A "chronic grief syndrome" then follows that can include anxieties about sexual problems, dyspareunia (difficult or painful coitus in women), promiscuity, infertility, and/or menstrual difficulties. Rejection of affected children may be reflected in overcompensation such as overprotectiveness and "medical shopping." Tips and Lynch (1968) also predict insidious changes in both the immediate family constellation and in extended families when certain relatives are labeled and rejected as carriers of "bad" genes.

A genetic diagnosis has been characterized as precipitating both acute and chronic stresses (Schild, 1966). The impact of the genetic diagnosis can be viewed as a crisis precipitant, with the initial focus centering on reproductive risks and potentially leading to psychological, social, and/or sexual conflicts and anxieties. The implications flowing from the reproductive decision may be further sources of severe stress at different points in the lifetimes of the individual and the family. One dynamic that may operate in these families has been described as a "shattered self-adequacy syndrome" in which the knowledge that one possesses a defective gene may cause a tremendous assault on the ego structure (Schild, 1966, p. 26). In a recent investigation, this dynamic was observed in many parents of children suffering from osteogenesis imperfecta* (Kiely et al., 1976). The researchers concluded that the insult to the parents' egos did indeed foster inadequate parental functioning. "Giving birth to a child with osteogenesis imperfecta was found to be initially devastating for parents who had no knowledge of the disease" (p. 414).

Shore (1975) and Kessler (1979) comment on the potentially penetrating effects of a genetic diagnosis on the ego. Shore (1975) has described this issue in terms of a "psychology of defectiveness." Kessler (1979) points out that while most diseases are experienced as ego-alien and are thus readily externalized, this is not generally the case for genetic diseases. Genetic disorders more often are experienced as the consequences of internal causes; the genes, which are in every cell of the body, are part of the self. Therefore, genetic diseases cannot be readily projected outward, "the entire person is experienced as defective . . . unable to diminish its threat via projection only increases the frightening powers of genetic disease" (p. 24).

Overall, there is little controversy that some individuals do have serious emotional repercussions as a result of genetic diagnoses. Disagreements arise, however, over how prevalent these reactions are and how much emphasis should be placed on looking for these severe consequences. One position postulates that the diagnostic impact is experienced profoundly, and psychotherapy is seen as the treatment of choice. Tips and Lynch (1968), for example, emphasize the need for psychological counseling; long-term psychotherapy for the individual and family is viewed as beneficial. An opposing view holds that psychological help should not become an integral part of genetic counseling. For example, Check (1980) has argued that trying to meet the clients' psychological needs dilutes the "main objective" of genetic counseling, which is to inform people about risk and enable them to make informed decisions about childbearing. Reality most likely lies between these two extreme positions—a view supported by others in the field. Fraser (1974), a major authority in the field of genetic counseling, takes issue with the "whole family concept" offered by Tips et al. (1964) in that it involves a psychiatric emphasis not needed by most clients. Fraser, although recognizing the need to be aware of potential psychological difficulties, contends that the effects of a genetic diagnosis have been greatly exaggerated.

Our own clinical experiences lead us to conclude that although personal concerns and problems certainly are significant concomitants of a genetic diagnosis, most clients do not become psychiatrically disturbed. They are not automatically, or even frequently, candidates for psychotherapy. Most clients have expectable, normal-for-the-situation dilemmas and concerns to which they apply their usual methods for coping. Clients seeking genetic counseling are often under stress, however. Their concerns may be *present related,* i.e., to the daily burdens of care and management for the affected person(s), or *future oriented,* to what fate holds in store for themselves or other family members. This situation resembles that faced by most families having members who have chronic illnesses or developmental or emotional disabilities. The pattern of responses to a genetic diagnosis may include shock, denial, anger, depression, and mourning—the frequent and normal reactions seen so often in situations of grief and loss (Featherstone, 1980; Golan, 1978; Olshansky, 1962; Simos, 1979; Solnit & Stark, 1961).

Many clients will be able to handle these stresses and cope effectively if they are provided with adequate information and support throughout the genetic counseling process. Other clients, however, find their existing coping strategies are ineffective in dealing with the novel genetic stresses. Prolonged denial or anger may block their ability to understand or accept the genetic facts. An extended period of depression may impair their ability to function in daily activities. In such cases, crisis intervention techniques and planned, short-term intervention are likely to prove effective in helping the majority of clients (Golan, 1978), with longer term psychotherapy indicated in only a small minority of cases.

Common Characteristics of Genetic Disorders

Given then that there is an expectable, general emotional reaction to the genetic diagnosis, in what ways, if any, is this reaction unique because of its genetic origins? There are two essential elements that explain the unique impact of a genetic diagnosis. First, despite the wide heterogeneity of genetic diseases, several common attributes of almost all genetic disorders are identifiable. These common characteristics inherently influence the social and psychological state of the affected individual and/or family. Second, it is the *special configuration* of these common features that elicits emotional reactions and upsets psychosocial functioning. The presence of one or even a few of these factors might not prove sufficient to precipitate emotional reactions in any unique way because of the genetic aspects of the situation. However, in the specific constellation of genetic features, a genetic diagnosis takes on a special import to many clients. *The genetic diagnosis, in general, defines a condition that is permanent, chronic, familial, complex, labeling, and threatening* (Schild, 1977a,b). These characteristics are weighted with significance in relation to the degree of illness, disability, and/or disfigurement stemming from the genetic defect, and to the self-concepts, perceptions, and value orientations of the involved individuals. The relative influence of these components of a genetic diagnosis are idiosyncratic to each case situation, but do play a part in each.

The *permanency* feature reflects the fact that the diagnosis is an irreversible actuality, a fixed attribute of the individual. Kessler (1979) contributes some important observations on this issue. He points out that whereas many diseases can be treated and the person restored to health, in a genetic situation, "the person knows . . . that the genotype cannot be changed. It is fixed for the duration of life . . . . There is a sense of fatalism, a hopelessness about the future, and a helplessness to alter natural laws over which the individual has no control" (p. 24).

Thus an accurately and firmly made genetic diagnosis is a lasting reality and as such can have a shattering effect on self-concepts. The insult to the ego and the way in which the genetic knowledge diminishes and/or changes self-esteem can be understood in terms of the concept of *genetic identity* (Schild, 1981). Genetic identity encompasses a psychological concept of self which derives from the inherited traits with which one is born. This genetic identity represents the sense of immortality evidenced in the continuation of family blood lines. In the organization of their genetic identities, individuals need to come to grips with the limitations as well as the strengths of their genetic endowments. It seems likely that a critical genetic aberration can compromise seriously the sense of self-adequacy and ego identity the individual needs in order to make a constructive psychological adaptation. On the other side, satisfaction with genetic structure and expression can enhance self-esteem. This may explain in part the strong desire of some adopted individuals to seek out their natural parents. By learning more about their heritage, a more complete sense of genetic identity becomes possible. However, the search for one's heritage may uncover unforeseen surprises such as a strong family history for a serious genetic disease.

Self-concepts need to be modified in the light of the revised genetic identity: "I am a carrier of Sickle-Cell Anemia," or "We are a PKU family." The intrinsic difference, permanently identified by the genetic diagnosis, now spotlights a uniqueness in the person that may be either accepted or perceived negatively by oneself and/or by others, and that may be inconvenient, discomforting, restricting, or demanding in nature. It is important to emphasize here that a genetic defect that is not seriously disabling, stigmatizing, or otherwise deleterious usually does not evoke such problems in genetic identity formation. This is especially true if the genetic defects are correctable, treatable, or readily disguised. However, it is important to keep in mind that even seemingly inconsequential disorders can be quite psychologically stressful, if distorted perceptions and meanings become attached to the minor defects.

Chronicity aspects of a genetic disorder stem from the irrefutable fact of its permanence, of its being a lifelong condition. The chronic nature of the genetic problem may be experienced as a threat at varying points in the life history of clients. For example, the genetic diagnosis may be threatening to developmental events such as marriage and childbearing. This holds true equally for carriers (who have not expressed the genetic defect symptomatically) or for extended kindred who have concerns, warranted or not, about reproductive risks. The chronic strains inherent in the management of the disease and/or in the burden of care required for the affected person also become realistic stresses for the caretakers, and out-of-home supports and services may be required.

A perhaps self-evident fact is that almost always a genetic diagnosis is also a *family diagnosis*. Family members are automatically included in the assessment of inheritance and of reproductive risks. They may also find that they themselves are "affected." Reproductive risks may emerge as a serious possibility. Some may learn that they face a significant chance for developing serious health problems in the future. Others may discover that they indeed have the disorder themselves, although it is expressed so mildly that it may never have been detected.

An illustration of the family implications of a genetic diagnosis is seen clearly in the following case situation.

> Infant Julie, 6 months, was referred for genetic evaluation with a tentative diagnosis of Pierre Robin Anomaly, a frequently benign, nongenetic problem involving underdevelopment of the lower jaw. A preclinic visit was made by the social worker to prepare the mother, Luci, for the clinic visit. Luci, a 19-year-old, single mother, was very concerned about the baby. She reported that the infant was failing to thrive, seemed sickly, and appeared delayed in her development. The family history revealed that Luci's two sisters, who were still living at home, had speech and hearing problems. Her mother also had a hearing problem. Julie's putative father had a medical history that was essentially negative.
>
> A shift in diagnosis occurred, however, when the geneticist examined Julie and Luci and obtained a family history. The new diagnosis of a genetic disorder, Treacher-Collins syndrome,* was made when the geneticist not only observed that Luci had a partial absence of her lower eyelids and skin tags in front of the ears[3] but also learned that Luci's mother and sisters had similar skin tags and other cardinal features of the syndrome (such as hearing problems). Thus at one fell swoop the diagnosis of this autosomal dominant disorder implicated the maternal grandmother, Luci, her two sisters, and the infant Julie.

A family diagnosis, especially if it puts members into jeopardy, can have a powerful impact on established interpersonal relationships. This impact can be either strengthening or disruptive in nature. Problems of carrier status and reproductive risks take on immediacy and importance; family planning decisions are influenced by these factors. Parents may draw closer together out of a sense of shared guilt and responsibility as when each carries the implicated recessive gene. Or, parents may be pulled apart when the genetic information is misused to meet other emotional and conflictual needs, as when blame is put on the partner with an altered dominant gene: "You're the one with bad blood"; "this has never happened in my family!"

Other significant problems may result from the *complexity* of the biological processes and of the genetic information embodied in the diagnosis. Very often, the data are beyond the level of scientific knowledge of the average client and his/her family. In addition to scientific information on physiological and biological factors, the genetic data are complicated further by the fact that reproductive risks are given in terms of probabilities. Many people have trouble understanding abstract concepts of probability and chance, and myths and fallacies often have a strong influence on risk-taking behaviors.

The inherent complexity of the genetic diagnosis also may pose obstacles to the clear communication of genetic information to clients. Investigations of client understanding of genetic information after genetic counseling indicate a rather uncertain level of comprehension of these complex data (see, for example, Black, 1979; Griffin et al., 1976; Leonard, Chase, & Childs, 1972; Sorenson et al., 1981). Confusion about the facts may increase anxieties and may have especially severe consequences if reproductive risks are understood incorrectly (Black, 1978).

Failure to understand complex genetic information is not necessarily the "fault" of the client, however. The counselor may fall prey to oversimplification, overcomplication, and/or carelessness in explication of the complex facts. What to tell? How much to tell? Whom to tell? When to tell? These are all important questions to be considered in the counseling activity. Since the ability to effect clear communication is contingent upon the emotional status and motivational level of the client, propitious timing and helping skills are essential. These factors are perhaps more crucial to the teaching-learning process necessary for effective communication of unfamiliar information than is the client's level of intellectual or educational achievement. Evidence in support of this latter issue has recently been reported by Sorenson et al. (1981). Their research findings refute the assumption that more educated clients are more likely to learn diagnostic and risk information provided in genetic counseling. On the contrary, these researchers concluded, "Clients with a graduate or college level education who entered counseling not knowing their diagnoses or risk, were no more likely to learn this in counseling than clients with a high school or junior high school level education" (p. 93).

Labeling is inevitable and necessary in order to facilitate detection, categorization, treatment, and prevention of genetic disorders. At the same time, labels also have the potential of carrying powerful connotations of deviance (Becker, 1973; Lemert, 1951; Rains, Kitsuse, Duster, & Friedson, 1975). Panides (1979) addresses this issue with his concept of "perinatal deviance." This concept describes any event, such as a genetic outcome, that varies from the normal perinatal sequence and is stress amplifying. Personal feelings of deviance, as well as stereotypical assumptions of others, may prove very stigmatizing to the family. Labeling incorporates notions of difference and thus may take on pejorative connotations; these can be used to promote adverse social attitudes, behaviors, or social policies. Because the labeling process often results in overgeneralizations, it can reinforce biases and stereotypes; as a result, labeling can promote exaggerated and/or inappropriate fears and reactions toward those who are labeled. Nevertheless, it is important to keep in mind that the labeling process appropriately focuses attention on the special needs of the diagnosed groups. Labeling can be used constructively to help affected persons deal realistically with the existence and the implications of their differences.

Finally, a genetic diagnosis is often *threatening* in nature. The diagnosis has a propensity to be a crisis precipitant because of the inherent threats to life and functioning. Serious genetic disorders often prognosticate a shortened life span (as in Marfan syndrome*) or early death (as in Tay-Sachs disease*). Degenerative disease processes in some genetic disorders may lead to seriously handicapping losses in physical and mental functioning (as seen in Huntington disease*). Threats to childbearing wishes and to family aspirations flow out of reproductive risks that are present and from the findings of prenatal diagnosis. The current life-style of the individual and/or the family may come under attack if the needs of the genetically affected family members cannot be met within the current mode of family functioning. On and on goes the list of potential stresses and threats; all areas of living are vulnerable in the face of the genetic diagnosis.

Crises Precipitated by Genetic Disorders

The significance of the common characteristics of the genetic diagnosis is that they often act as crisis precipitants. Typically, the intensity of the crisis responses of clients depends largely on the meanings affected individuals and family members attach to the genetic diagnosis. These meanings, in turn, are reflective of feelings and attitudes about the perceived losses or threats inferred by the diagnosis. Personal disruptions may occur in value systems, interpersonal relationships, and in self-concepts. Equally important are the crises that are situational in nature. A personal crisis for clients may be induced if any of the following resources are unavailable, inaccessible, or unsuitable: finances, medical care, nursing services, health facilities, child care, transportation, respite care programs, schooling, special training, or rehabilitation programs. Undoubtedly the reader can add many more items to this listing.

Crises may reflect reactions to acute events or the build up of chronic strain. The chronicity of genetic disorders often stresses the tolerance and patience of individuals who are dealing daily with the demands of the genetic disease. Stresses pile up for clients who need to search out and accommodate complex institutions that provide the needed resources and services. When the tensions and strains of addressing special needs are imposed on the ordinary and common needs of everyday living, the challenge may become overwhelming and thrust clients into situational crises.

In order to resolve or to cope successfully with the crises that are evoked by genetic diagnoses, clients are faced with a series of psychosocial tasks for mastery. These psychological and situational tasks have been identified by Schild (1977b):

1. Reaffirmation of self-worth, involving the reorganization of self-concepts.
2. Acceptance of a new genetic identity and changed body image.
3. Acceptance of the inherent limitations of the genetic diagnosis, including implied losses such as the loss of a desired, healthy, normal child.
4. Adjustment to felt difference or deviancy, including coping with social stigma.
5. Mastery of new social roles, person-with-a-genetic-defect, parent-of-a-genetically-defective-child.
6. Accommodating special needs dictated by the genetic disorder in a way that does not interfere with normal growth and development.
7. Obtaining treatment and carrying out medical recommendations.
8. Obtaining specialized services to meet specific needs such as respite care and special education. This requires the assumption of client roles in relation to appropriate community agencies.
9. Altering life-style to accommodate special needs and problems.
10. Meeting basic needs (normalization) and participating in regular programs (mainstreaming) at the same time that special needs are addressed.

These psychological and situational tasks are often burdensome for clients, yet their successful mastery leads to more effective adaptation. It is for these tasks that clients often may need to have crisis help, supportive counseling, and at times active advocacy assistance in obtaining mandated services.

PSYCHOLOGICAL ASPECTS OF REPRODUCTIVE RISKS

Although it is beyond the scope of this book to explore the multiple motivations underlying the decision of couples to become parents,[4] it seems clear that couples who seek genetic counseling about reproductive risks often are experiencing apprehension and conflict. Kessler (1979) highlights this fact:

In sum, the reasons underlying the desire for parenthood are usually complex and in many, if not all instances, the motivations are not entirely within the person's consciousness. In the best of circumstances, the needs of the two persons involved probably contain some conflicting or ambivalent elements. *When procreation entails a risk for a child with a genetic disorder, the ambivalence may be intensified* [italics added]. (p. 26)

Generally, couples requesting genetic counseling have a family history of genetic abnormality, have already produced a defective child, or have been identified in some form of genetic screening as at increased risk for conceiving an offspring with a genetic disorder. The genetic information asked for thus can be at the same time wanted and feared, helpful and unhelpful, gratifying and disappointing, supportive and discouraging.

The ambiguity commonly contained in the genetic-risk information serves to compound the ambivalence of prospective parents. Even the most precise figures will never result in predictive certainty. Given, for example, the relatively high risk of 50% in each pregnancy of transmitting an autosomal dominant disorder such as Huntington disease or Marfan syndrome, there still is no unequivocal prediction of the presence or absence of the genetic defect in future offspring. Clients still face a situation of "iffiness," uncertainty, and risk. Even in cases where accurate diagnosis is possible in prenatal diagnosis, uncertainty exists prior to the receipt of the test results. Further ambiguity emerges when the disorder in question has an uncertain or variable impact, as seen in the discovery of a fetus with a XYY karyotype during "routine" screening for Down syndrome. Personal morals and ethics also may complicate the decision to continue or abort the pregnancy.

The way in which information on reproductive risks is understood or perceived depends on the psychological needs of the clients to bear children. Kessler (1979) points out that strongly motivated and weakly motivated couples may use selective hearing or distort recurrence risk figures to support their respective needs. As a result, the same genetic-risk figures may seem negligible to one couple and enormous to another. By the same token, the perceptions of burden of care are idiosyncratic and based on the psychological needs, attitudes, and feelings of the involved individuals. The perceptions of reproductive risks are tempered and influenced by the perceptions about the burden of the disorder. High risks may be chanced if the burden of care is minimal and vice versa.

When scientific knowledge and technology were less advanced, it may have been easier for people to make reproductive decisions. Despite the universal fear held by most pregnant women, and presumably by most prospective fathers as well, of producing a defective child, most people are able to defend themselves psychologically and to trust that this will not happen to them. Having a child is viewed usually in the context of risks of everyday life. The advances in human genetics, such as screening and prenatal diagnostic procedures, are changing this perspective, however. Today many people are called upon to choose risky courses of action that previously have been seen as routine, minimally conflicted decisions for which there were no options from which to choose. Some examples of such areas of uncertainty that can have an effect on reproductive resolutions include: (1) whether or not to have a child in the face of genetic information indicating a "small" but increased risk of serious defect in the offspring; (2) whether or not to work in a well-paying job requiring exposure to chemicals that have been shown to produce chromosome damage and to cause a low but statistically significant risk of future cancer or birth defects in offspring; or (3) whether or not to undergo prenatal testing and abort any male fetus because of the 50% chance that it has a serious X-linked genetic defect that cannot be diagnosed specifically in utero (Black, 1981).

It seems likely that prior risk-taking behavior patterns will influence the way in which people make decisions about reproductive risks. The evidence from genetic counseling confirms that decision making under conditions of uncertainty is a highly subjective and complex process.[5] Decision making in the face of ambiguity and chance is vulnerable to numerous cognitive, as well as emotional, biases that can result in dysfunctional resolutions. It is also clear that this kind of decision making is likely to be an emotionally stressful experience. Clinical research on coping and adaptation shows that one's appraisal of a potentially stressful event is influenced by the ambiguity of the threat and by one's resources in countering it (Lazarus, 1966).

The cognitive demands involved in making decisions in the face of uncertain risks stand with equal significance alongside the emotional stresses imposed by such situations. Social psychological research has begun to identify flaws and limitations in human information processing that shape decision making (see, for example, Abelson, 1976; Hamilton, 1976; Janis & Mann, 1977; Langer, 1975; Slovic, Fischoff, & Lichtenstein, 1976; Tversky & Kahneman, 1981). Information processing is distorted, for instance, by the way the data are presented; by distracting, irrelevant issues; by faulty stereotypes and categories; etc. A major limitation in processing information about genetic uncertainty is the decision maker's illusion about probabilities. Even those who are sophisticated in the technical use of statistics and probabilities show frequent and consistent biases in their practical use of probabilities in decision making (Tversky & Kahneman, 1981). For example, there is the familiar gambler's fallacy in which there is the belief that chance is a self-correcting process in which a deviation in one direction is likely to be followed by a deviation in the opposite direction: "Those doctors said the odds were one in four that we would have a retarded child. Since we've had three normal children already, we'd better stop now before the odds catch up with us." Similar problems are found in the ability to accept the notion of probabilistic independence. People tend to estimate that the coin-flipping sequence H-T-H-T-T-H is more likely than H-H-H-T-T-T or H-H-H-H-T-H: "We've already had our PKU child so the next child will be normal." Individuals at other times show difficulties in using information about prior baseline probabilities; disregarding the data which may show probabilities greater or less than 50%, they tend to see the chances of the outcome as 50-50. People may prefer to believe that they have an even chance of winning out.

"Availability" biases are another powerful factor in increasing the perceived risk of individuals who have had genetic counseling about recurrence risks in reproduction. These refer to situations in which people assess the probability of an event by the ease with which instances or occurrences can be brought to mind. Research indicates that people tend to disregard sound evidence of low risks if possible unfavorable outcomes are brought to their attention. This is especially true if the ensuing disasters are easy to imagine. In one study of parents of children with Down syndrome, it was shown that many parents indicated the recurrence risk was higher than they had imagined it might be. This perception appeared to be heavily influenced by the sudden exposure of these parents to the concrete realities of their children's genetic disorder (Black, 1978, 1981).

On the basis of such research findings, it becomes clear that notions of high or low risks are subjectively determined and unique for each individual. When one sees and personally experiences events that are said to be quite rare, it is extremely difficult, if not impossible, to view "objectively" one's risk as low. One parent concluded:

> Statistics scare us. We had a low probability for a miscarriage, a low probability of having a child with a heart malformation, a low probability of the child surviving the operation, and a low probability of placental retention after his birth, and they all happened. (Lippman-Hand & Fraser, 1979b, p. 118)

Lippman-Hand and Fraser (1979a) identified that a frequent pattern was for parents to translate factual rates into "binary" form. Parents emphasized that "no matter the size of the recurrence rate, something can happen—a one in the numerator never disappears no matter the size of the denominator, and this 'one' could be the counselee's child" (p. 332). Uncertainty is thereby maximized, because, in the parent's mind, the risk has become essentially 50-50. "Will I have an affected child? Well, it either will or will not happen" (p. 332).

Much of genetic counseling in the past was founded on the belief that clients will use a "rational" decision-making process once they are in possession of the genetic facts and figures. Strong evidence points to the reverse situation being true when people face decision making under extreme uncertainty. The Nobel Prize winner, Herbert Simon (1976) hypothesized that the decision maker often lacks the "wits to maximize" and instead chooses a "satisficing" approach which provides a course of action that is "good enough." He suggests that because people are of "bounded or limited rationality" they are unable to comprehend all the possible implications of their decisions, to obtain all the necessary information about the available alternatives, to estimate probabilities, or to work out preference orderings for the many different alternatives.

Recent research by Lippman-Hand and Fraser (1979a,b,c,d) provides striking support for the related notion that rationality becomes irrelevant when facing genetic decisions based on enormous uncertainties. According to these researchers, in order to use a rational process in reproductive decision making, three major questions need to be clearly answered: (1) "How likely am I to have an affected child?" (2) "What will it be like if it happens?" and (3) "How will others react to my choice?" (1979a, p. 330). Their research revealed, however, that these questions rarely are able to be answered with any certainty. As a result, the major decision-making strategy adopted by parents involved the development of various "scenarios" in which the parents imagined the possible outcomes of the event. The uncertainty and ambiguity of the situations provided free rein to their imaginations, allowing them to test their emotional responses as they "tried out the worst." Through the use of their imaginary scenarios, parents seemed to be searching for a "least-lose" or "satisficing" alternative in which maximum loss would be acceptable and thus allow them to take the risk of future pregnancies. The parental responses and reproductive choices represented the attempts to limit or neutralize the uncertainties facing parents and the parental perceptions of the coping required to deal with the imposed problems.

The research cited focuses on *how* reproductive choices are determined rather than on *what* decisions are made; it vividly illustrates the importance of gaining more knowledge and fuller understanding of the psychological processes involved in coping with reproductive risks. Chapter 5 examines the implications for practice of these coping processes.

IMPACT OF AMNIOCENTESIS AND ABORTION FOR GENETIC REASONS

The few studies in prenatal diagnosis that have examined psychological responses to and decision making involved in amniocentesis and abortion for genetic indications reveal that the potentially negative psychological ramifications of these procedures merit consideration. Anxiety, guilt, doubt, and ambivalence have been described in women undergoing amniocentesis (Blumberg, Golbus, & Hanson, 1975; Fletcher, 1972,

1973; Robinson, Tennes, & Robinson, 1975). Robinson, Tennes, and Robinson (1975) concluded in their study of the possible impact of amniocentesis on mothers and the resulting normal offspring that the prenatal procedure was accepted easily and was viewed as an appropriate part of prenatal care by women 35 years of age or older who had no previously affected offspring. However, mothers with a previously affected child tended to have more conflict over possible abortions, higher anxiety about the test, and needed more intensive counseling. The period marked with highest anxiety appears to be the time after the test is done and before the results are known. Blumberg, Golbus, and Hanson (1975) examined 13 families in which abortions were performed when the fetus was found to be affected or to be a male at risk for an X-linked recessive disorder. The most frequent response to the abortion was depression; the actual incidence was thought to be as high as 92% among the women and 82% among the fathers in the families studied. Two families had marital separations during the pregnancies in question, which the researchers believed were related to the genetic circumstances. In two other families, brief separations occurred following the abortion, reflecting the powerful stresses present in these experiences.

In a study on the anxiety engendered by amniocentesis, Beeson and Golbus (1979) reported that there were significant elevations in anxiety documented just prior to the procedure and then later just prior to receiving test results. As in the Lippman-Hand and Fraser (1979a,b,c,d) study, this research focused on the *how* and not the *what* of the decision making on the issue. Subjects were found to cope with the anxiety in terms of their perceptions of the amniocentesis situation. A common stratagem was the "suspension" of pregnancy by devices that hid physical changes, not wearing maternity clothes and not discussing the pregnancy. The researchers believe the anxiety levels represented clients' perceptions of the event and their evaluations of the threats posed by the situation in which they found themselves. Even aside from the issue of the prenatal diagnostic procedure itself, Beeson and Golbus (1979) found that the pregnancies of the amniocentesis patients were viewed as highly emotionally charged. Among women over 35 years of age, pregnancies included those that were unplanned, those that followed difficulties in conception or one or more miscarriages, and those that were the product of late marriages. The researchers observed that certain factors in particular seemed to undermine the parents' confidence in their ability to reproduce a healthy fetus. These included: (1) a previous child with a chromosomal disorder; (2) a history of repeated miscarriages, spotting during pregnancy; (3) a history of poor health in the mother; and (4) primagravity (first pregnancy). In contrast, the women who experienced low anxiety showed a different profile; they: (1) had one or more healthy children; (2) had a clear resolution to abort the pregnancy if the results were abnormal;

(3) had a supportive husband; (4) were in a planned pregnancy; (5) had had no prior miscarriages; and (6) had one or more friends who had had amniocentesis. These profiles are helpful for assessing those clients who are most vulnerable to more severe psychological distress and who might be most in need of supportive counseling.

In considering the above cited research and its contributions to a better understanding of the anxiety engendered by amniocentesis, it is important to bear in mind that Beeson and Golbus (1979) did not conclude that the anxiety observed at the time of amniocentesis was predictive of later anxieties. It is also not known how, if at all, this experience alters or effects the longer term psychosocial functioning of women undergoing amniocentesis.

Fletcher (1972) studied 25 couples who had been involved in genetic counseling, had had amniocentesis performed, and who either gave birth or had the pregnancy aborted. Three major periods of decision making were identified: (1) the decision to seek genetic counseling and amniocentesis; (2) decisions made after amniocentesis and after learning the diagnosis; and (3) decisions made after the abortion, sterilization, or birth. Fletcher (1972) describes a phenomenon of "cosmic guilt" as characteristic of these parents in which there is an unusual sense of shame and guilt associated with genetic disease. Furthermore, Fletcher speculates that parents underwent a "moral suffering" as they struggled with their conflicts, duties, and changing perception of parenthood (pp. 464–468). The most acute personal suffering was found expectably to follow a positive diagnosis; acute conflict and pain were experienced over abortion and sterilization decisions. Fletcher advances the interesting thesis that there is a difference in the bonding process that occurs between parent and tested child as a result of amniocentesis, because the active parent role begins early in the pregnancy. "Assurance of the health of the child releases parental care, planning, and symbolic activity usually reserved for birth" (1972, p. 477). However, the fact that the parents who have aborted a fetal sib or, indeed, have even considered prenatal abortion of a delivered healthy child may carry inherent psychological threats to the parent-child relationship with other siblings at some future point. Fletcher (1972) concluded that the results of his study

> would support a hypothesis that parents are aware of some alteration in the formation of trust in their relations to tested and untested children, due to the abortion issue; further, this alteration is seen as justified in the light of known risks about their childbearing. (p. 478)

While Fletcher's main thrust is on exploration of moral issues, his research adds significantly to our understanding of the complex psychological dynamics involved in amniocentesis and abortion for genetic reasons. The evidence on anxiety in amniocentesis is far from conclusive. Contrary to what had been assumed, Ashery (1977) reported evidence that indicated amniocentesis was not necessarily a crisis situation. In fact, in her study, the subjects found the procedure to be less disturbing than classical crisis situations that they had previously experienced. "The population was not found to be either unstable, extremely suggestible, ambivalent, or inappropriately emotional concerning amniocentesis" (p. 40). Despite these general findings, Ashery estimated that approximately 10–15% of the study population would need some level of emotional support and suggested the following situations as indications for involvement by a social worker: (1) couples exhibiting extreme anxiety; (2) cases in which a positive diagnosis of a genetic indication is made; and (3) cases in which the physician requires (and requests) consultation about how to approach a couple in the delivery of genetic information. As Ashery acknowledged, the generalizability of these results is uncertain because the study was limited to one clinic, with a fairly homogeneous population; only two couples had high-risk figures and only one positive diagnosis, which did evoke a crisis situation, was made. Much more research, using larger, more representative samples, will be required before more conclusive generalizations about responses to amniocentesis can be made. It seems reasonable to project, however, that the easy acceptance by women of "routine" amniocentesis, that is for those 35 years of age and older with no previous history of problems, will continue to grow. This acceptance seems to be the result of increased education about the procedure, favorable publicity reported in the lay press, and the medical profession's shift to viewing amniocentesis as a standard rather than experimental medical procedure.

IMPACT OF THE GENETIC COUNSELING SITUATION

In addition to the potentially stressful features of genetic disorders, there are also potential difficulties that can arise out of the experience of the genetic evaluation and genetic counseling process. For many individuals, the genetic work-up or evaluation is part of the visit to the genetic counseling clinic, and all too often it is a time when clients feel stressed and under scrutiny by professionals. Their sense of difference becomes exaggerated as questions probe areas related to family abnormalities and illnesses. We have discussed at some length the stresses imposed by the complexities of genetic information and the frequent obscurities and ambiguities characterizing the diagnosis. Clients may respond with awe, confusion, and bewilderment to the professionals whom they do not know and to the information and procedures that they may not really comprehend. Sometimes, as described in Chapter 3, a diagnosis can be made primarily by visual inspection and characterization of a specific malformation syndrome (see, for example, Smith, 1976). For some clients this can be disturbing. "How can the doctor tell just by looking?" is a commonly heard complaint. Clinical experience with genetic clients shows that they need time to share their concerns, to articulate feelings in a trusting milieu, to learn new ways to master their troubles, and to obtain and identify needed services. These needs often cannot be met in the typical genetic counseling model of "short-term interaction between two parties who have only just met, are barely acquainted and will have little, if any further dealings with each other" (Golden, Davis, & Leary, 1981, p. 124).

In many instances, for example, newborns or individuals hospitalized for apparently nongenetic reasons, the genetic work-up often begins in the hospital ward or neonatal unit. In such cases, as in formal genetic counseling situations, research indicates that the evaluation process can be a difficult and painful experience. For example, several studies (Daniels & Berg, 1968; Drotar, Baskiewicz, Irvin, Kennell, & Klaus, 1975; Johns, 1971) have shown that parents viewing their malformed baby do not often focus on the defects; to the contrary, seeing the infant sometimes allays anxieties that had magnified the unseen defects in the parents' eyes. However, when the geneticists begin to pore over an individual child in a search for features suggestive of a genetic syndrome, a difficult and stressful situation may be precipitated. As one parent stated, "They looked her over like a specimen." Or in the words of another parent:

> it was a strange, overwhelming experience—to see your child looked at like a piece of meat. I don't look at her that way. I remember one doctor looking at her and saying her eyes were too far apart—the most beautiful eyes you ever saw—and for someone to look at her and be judging how far apart they are. (Black, 1980a, p. 144)

The clients' expectations about genetic counseling may be a source of potential stress. People quite naturally look to genetic diagnosis and counseling for answers to their questions. Will we have normal children? Will it happen again? These are frequent and appropriate concerns. Yet, as we have described, the "answers" in terms of reproductive risks can only be given in hedging, probabilistic terms. The all too frequent uncertainties about diagnoses and genetic etiologies only serve to compound the inherent ambiguity of genetic counseling situations. As one parent, reflecting on the usefulness of genetic counseling, stated: "I didn't discover anything—no definite answers. Maybe that's why I felt let down" (Lippman-Hand & Fraser, 1979c, p. 59).

The prognosis for an affected individual becomes another source of uncertainty and stress. The naming of a genetic etiology may not necessarily point the way for cure or treatment. Many known syndromes vary greatly in the severity of their expression, and the future trajectory of an individual's genetic disease may not be predictable in infancy or in the early stages of the disorder (Strauss & Glaser, 1975). Research identifies that to the extent that genetic counseling does not supply answers, it complicates the issues parents have to consider without presenting any clear solutions to their problems (Lippman-Hand & Fraser, 1979c, p. 59).

NEEDS FOR SOCIAL WORK SERVICES

Earlier in this chapter we suggested that genetic disorders and diagnoses can precipitate crises for clients and that there are both situational and psychological tasks that need to be mastered for successful crisis resolutions. We turn our attention now to the service needs that are generated by these crises. As we look at the specific needs for services that arise out of both acute and chronic strains associated with serious genetic disorders, we note many similarities to the needs of individuals and families with developmental disabilities or other severe, chronic illnesses and handicaps. The needs for social work of clients with genetic problems have been identified as follows (Schild, 1977a):

1. crisis help,
2. anticipatory guidance,
3. linkage to support systems,
4. family-life education,
5. a fixed point for service,
6. family planning,
7. provision of material and environmental resources,
8. supportive counseling,
9. advocacy.

Obviously, not all clients will have all of these needs. However, a significant proportion of clients are likely to develop needs for many if not most of these services at one time or another.

Crisis help recognizes that by definition people who are thrust into crisis situations are likely to be somewhat overwhelmed and possibly immobilized. Families experiencing genetic crises may require help in learning to cope with the disorganizing effects of the unusual stresses and the threats that are perceived. Clients may need support in learning to adjust to their changed situations and in developing new adaptive behaviors to cope with continuing problems.

Anticipatory guidance follows from the crisis perspective and is aimed at the prevention of undue problems. Clients expressing considerable anxieties about future concerns can benefit from knowing, to the greatest extent possible, what to expect. Anticipatory guidance thus can reduce anxiety by giving clients a way to share some of their fears and misgivings. It also helps by introducing a reality orientation in which clients can have the opportunity to prepare and rehearse for future developments.

Linkages to support systems are needed by many people who feel isolated by their genetic disorders. In fact, since many serious genetic disorders are so rare, there is a reality to the aloneness and alienation that clients frequently experience. Potential sources of support include: social service agencies, various health programs and agencies, self-help groups, as well as the natural helping networks (Collins & Pancoast, 1976) created by family and friends.

Needs arise frequently for *environmental and material resources* such as financial assistance, respite care, homemaker services, home health services, and child care. Many clients cannot cope financially with expensive medical and special services required in the care and management of certain genetically affected individuals. Other material needs, although not unlike those of all families, often are magnified in the case of long-term, disabling disorders. Adequate environmental support and resources are essential requirements for positive family functioning.

A *fixed-point of service* is important for case management and for availability of recurrent help as it arises. Clients often find the complexities of bureaucratic service systems difficult to manage. Optimal management of many genetic disorders frequently requires multiple services such as medical, educational, and financial assistance provided by a variety of different agencies. Making essential linkages with the necessary resources and coordinating them to avoid duplication of services are complicated tasks for even the most sophisticated clients. In addition, the chronic nature of genetic disorders implies the need for a continuum of services over the lifetime of genetic clients. Genetic counseling, for example, may be indicated at various developmental stages after the point of initial diagnosis.

Family-life education is important to help families derive maximum satisfaction and function effectively as they cope with the special needs of disabled family member(s). Parents of mentally retarded or physically disabled children may tend to overprotect the child and then face conflicts over matters of discipline. These parents are likely to benefit from education in how to provide disciplined structure for their children. When an affected adult is no longer able to carry out previous responsibilities, family members may need assistance in learning new roles and methods of relating to each other and the outside world.

Family planning services are often required by clients struggling with reproductive dilemmas. Complicated emotional issues are involved in making decisions about alternatives to natural childbearing such as adoption and artificial insemination, and long-term consequences of such decisions require careful consideration. Abortion rarely represents a choice that is free of conflict, and social work assistance is useful in helping clients weigh their values and goals in relation to that option.

Supportive counseling is needed by clients who are emotionally stressed, perplexed, and, somewhat overwhelmed by the seeming enormity of certain genetic situations. Such clients are likely to benefit from empathic help for emotional concerns and from clarification of the pertinent medical and genetic information. It is crucial for individuals to feel that they do not have to struggle alone with the burdens of the genetic disorder.

The last, but equally important, need of clients is for *advocacy* on their behalf when their rights are abrogated or threatened. As much as possible, clients should be assisted in learning effective strategies for advocating for themselves. But the social worker will need to assume a more active role as advocate with appropriate individuals and/or agencies in a client's situation. Advocacy efforts also should concern themselves with the collective needs of various client groups, with attention directed to needed changes in organizational and governmental policies and procedures.

Genetic clients are confronted with: (1) acute crises, relating to the initial diagnosis or identification of genetic defects, and (2) chronic strains, resulting from recurrent situations activated by critical concerns and events stemming from the genetic defect. The intensity and range of needs expressed will depend specifically on the severity of the genetic disorder, the severity of the threats implied, the meanings that are given by clients to the event, and the nature of the personalities involved. Although severe emotional reactions may be precipitated by genetic events, such reactions are not the norm. Most reactions and needs of individuals are more accurately viewed as "normal-for-the-crisis" responses.

Social workers have the professional expertise to address the psychosocial issues that research and clinical experience have begun to identify as pertinent to the impact of genetic disorders. Many of the needs of clients require helping activities that focus on problems of interpersonal relationships, psychological functioning, and environmental transactions; all are activities that legitimately fall into the domain of social work practice. In the next chapter we focus on some of the specific practice implications of genetic concerns and problems. As the preceding review of service needs indicates, the practice challenges span the range of skills available to the professional social worker.

NOTES

1. These data were learned in the course of a home visit by the clinical social worker. The confusion held by the family about the genetic information was shared with the clinical geneticist and the orthopedist involved in the case. A return clinic visit was scheduled immediately to clarify the genetic facts for this family.

2. A useful review, *Social and Psychological Aspects of Genetic Disorders*, has recently been compiled by the National Center for Education in Maternal and Child Health, 3520 Prospect Street, Washington, DC 20007.

3. These skin tags are small, benign skin growths usually located just in front of the external ear.

4. Recommended readings on this subject include Fox (1982) and Pohlman (1969).

5. The following discussion of risk taking is drawn largely from Black (1981).

5

Perspectives on Clinical Practice

Social work is generic, it is also specific. The common values, knowledge, and skills are applied to specific situations. (Northen, 1982, p. 10)

GENERAL CONSIDERATIONS

This chapter addresses issues and needs pertinent to clinical social work practice in genetics. Before moving directly into that discussion, it is important to delineate the framework of clinical social work practice on which this discussion is based. Our view of the purpose, focus, and principles governing practice in direct services is articulated most closely in the recently proposed definition of clinical social work practice suggested by the National Association of Social Workers (NASW) (Cohen, 1980):

The practice of clinical social work involves a wide range of psychosocial services to individuals, families, and small groups in relation to a variety of human problems of living. Such practice may be carried out under both private and public auspices. It is concerned with the assessment of interaction between the individual's biological, psychological, and social experience which provides a guide for clinical intervention. Clinical social work, therefore, may involve intervention in the social situation as well as the person situation. Intervention in both the social situation and the person situation are valued approaches in clinical social work practice. At least three major principles by which clinical social work produces change or maintenance of function can be identified. Such goals may be reached through the interpersonal relationship with the clinician; they can be brought about through alterations in the social situation; and they can be brought about through alterations of relationships with significant others in the life space of the individual. Personal satisfaction and improved social functioning are both important ends; neither can be ignored or imputed to be one of shallow consequence. (p. 26)

This definition highlights the distinguishing feature of social work which is its professional concern with the social context in which individual and family problems occur and change. The focus reflects the profession's historical commitment to the person-situation formulation (Germain, 1979). This focus guides clinical practice in genetics as well; sights are targeted on what is taking place in the dynamic transaction between the client and her/his genetic situation.

The attention to the relationship between individuals and their social milieu has been described as an "ecological unit of attention" (Meyer, 1976). Flowing directly out of the principles of ecology, it emphasizes the adaptive fit between organisms and their environment. What is construed by "psychosocial functioning" are the ways individuals behave in adapting to their interpersonal (social) relations and the social conditions and situations (environments) that exist in their living worlds. For clients who have genetic problems and concerns, the adaptive goodness-of-fit achieved in social relationships and in social conditions often depends, at least to some degree, on the nature of their genetic disorder. As noted in Chapter 4, psychosocial functioning is vulnerable to intrapsychic, interpersonal, and environmental factors causing stress, threat, and disruption. Hence, the ecological perspective and the person-situation concept are conspicuously appropriate for clinical social work practice in relation to genetic concerns.

Goals of Practice

The essential purpose of the social work profession has been seen as one of individualizing need and providing for the growth and development of people in society (Meyer, 1976). The defined purpose to which the practice of clinical social work must be functionally related has been identified as "the maintenance and enhancement of psychosocial functioning of individuals, families, and small groups by maximizing the availability of needed intrapersonal, interpersonal, and societal resources" (Cohen, 1980, p. 30). The goals of clinical practice in genetics fit naturally into those of the social work profession as a whole, and of clinical social work practice itself.

> The basic objectives of social work intervention, where the focus of attention is the genetic concern, is the same regardless of the practice setting. The goal is to help the person and/or family prevent or resolve life problems flowing out of the dislocations and disturbances evoked by the diagnosis and/or presence of a genetic defect. The major aim of genetic social work is to improve the quality of life of involved individuals despite the limitations and liabilities imposed by the genetic problem; in this sense, the goal of genetic

social work is but a specific extension of the purpose of the social work profession itself. (Schild, 1977a, pp. 6-7)

The stated purpose of the profession and the ecological perspective have important implications for the nature of the functions to be undertaken in social work. "The most prevalent view is that enhancement, prevention, and remediation are all appropriate functions for social work" (Northen, 1982, p. 15). The goals of clinical social work in genetics incorporate all of these functions. The aim of heightening the quality of life of genetically affected clients coincides with the profession's concern with the promotion of opportunities for the enhancement of potentials and prevention of problems.

Unitary Approach to Practice

Although less agreement prevails in social work on the nature of an integrated or unitary approach to practice, the educational trend by 1980 has reflected strivings to evolve a unified theory for professional practice (Northen, 1982). We concur with Northen's thesis that the needs or problems of the client should determine the mode(s) of service. This requires that the social worker have the ability to utilize individual, family, group, and community approaches in purposeful and planful ways. Clinical experience in genetics has demonstrated that an integrated practice approach most aptly addresses many expressed needs of clients. The intense, emotional reactions and situational difficulties that can affect an individual with a genetic disorder and her/his family may signal far differing modes of helping interventions. A case in point is that of the Smith family, who illustrate the importance of services at the levels of individual, family, and community:

Mrs. Smith, 40, and her son, Andrew, 9, were diagnosed in the genetics clinic as having Marfan syndrome.* The social-situational assessment identified several immediate needs for service:

1. individual counseling for Mrs. Smith to help her in understanding the autosomal dominant transmission and her status as also affected by Marfan syndrome; for Andrew to assist him in adjusting to his physical appearance (see also 3 below);
2. family counseling for Mr. and Mrs. Smith and Andrew as well as Joan, 11, about the trajectory of the disorder, especially in regard to the mother's current eye and cardiac problems and Andrew's serious scoliosis; with special attention to be given to the implications for functioning of the family unit and reactions of the unaffected family members.

3. work in the community with school personnel around the school problems Andrew was experiencing seemingly as a result of his poor self-esteem and unsatisfactory peer relationships; both apparently derived from self-consciousness about his extreme height and the awkward appearance caused by his scoliosis;
4. help with financial stresses related to medical care; and
5. identification of and reaching out to kindred at risk of also being affected and who therefore could benefit from genetic counseling services.

Possible future service needs included:

1. helping the family to cope with the progressive manifestations of the disorder and the attendant stresses and problems that would likely be evoked; and
2. assisting in anticipatory preparation for the possibly shortened life span of the mother.

Clinical experience also has shown the significant benefit of group services to those clients who face rare and serious genetic disorders. It is not uncommon to have affected individuals express a desire to meet others who have their disease. Knowing others who share similar concerns and challenges can be not only supporting but also empowering for clients who feel alone and helpless in the face of their disorder. A graphic example of this was seen recently on national television when three families who have a child with progeria* publicly shared the significant meaning attached to their coming together for the first time. As discussed in more detail later in this chapter, social workers in genetics services have demonstrated the significance of addressing these felt needs by organizing and providing group services. Examples include: educational and support groups for parents of children with PKU* (Schild, 1964; Harold, personal communication, 1982); for teenage PKU patients (Harold, personal communication, 1982); for individuals with dwarfism (Weiss, 1977); for mothers of daughters with Turner syndrome* (Plumridge, personal communication, 1982); for adolescents with sickle cell anemia* (Conyard, Krishnamurthy, & Dosik, 1980; LePontois, 1975); and for spouses of individuals with Huntington disease (Miller, 1976).

Principles for Practice

The principles which are accepted generally by the social work profession as guiding general clinical social work practice apply equally to direct services in genetics. These principles are identified in NASW's proposed definition for clinical practice (Cohen, 1980):

1. Clinical assessment is based on the biopsychosocial aspects of the person, the environment, and the interrelatedness between the two, including the nature of the resources in both.
2. Intervention, planning, and goal setting are based upon clinical assessment, relevant theory, and client agreement, addressed to the client's unique situation and not limited by professional preference or expertise of the worker.
3. Clinical assessment is an ongoing process that may result in alteration of goals, or the treatment mode, and of services of assistance.
4. Evaluation of the effectiveness of the helping process is required.
5. Clinical social work has the responsibility of documenting deficiencies in resources or harmful conditions for clients and initiating change by making these conditions known to professional and institutional systems.

The social-situational assessment, including the social history and environmental context, may be crucial in making a genetic diagnosis or in determining how best to impart genetic advice and information. In one not untypical situation, the medical resident reported during a clinic staffing, ''no problems in the pregnancy.'' This was an incorrect statement, as the social worker tactfully pointed out, inasmuch as the father suspected the mother of infidelity and did not believe the child was his; a problematic pregnancy indeed, especially in terms of the genetic implications of the data.

Intervention strategies may be needed at different levels simultaneously and may reflect a variety of activities necessary to accomplish the tasks generated by the very nature of the genetic disorders. For instance, a family with PKU often requires services from a physician, psychologist, nutritionist, and educational counselor to meet the needs of the child. The family may benefit from assistance in dealing with the child's behavioral problems and with the stresses placed on the family members as a result of managing the extremely restrictive dietary treatment. Siblings and other relatives may benefit from genetic counseling about reproductive risks. Adult women who have PKU in particular should receive genetic counseling on the increased risks associated with childbearing and the availability of special monitoring should they become pregnant. The many participating agencies and service providers often may become overlapping, confusing, and even counterproductive. Thus, in order to carry out a myriad of tasks defined by the social situation and genetic problem, the social worker will be called upon to employ a variety of helping strategies, including linkage, consultation, collaboration, counseling, advocacy, case management.

The following case illustrates this mix of worker activities and tasks:

The birth of a male infant with Down syndrome had a profound effect on his parents, Joe and Sara Carlin. They felt incapable of loving, much less rearing, a retarded child and believed that a retarded sibling would be detrimental to their other three children (ages 7, 4, and 3). The Carlins, both health professionals, knew many of the medical staff involved in the delivery of the baby and were angered by the negative reactions of their professional colleagues when they decided to place the infant out of their home. The Carlins felt their decision for placement was not atypical; they did not believe that their professional training placed on them a greater responsibility to accept an abnormal child. Indeed, they thought the reactions of their colleagues were hypocritical, for had prenatal testing been done, the diagnosis made, and an elective abortion performed, the likely response would have been a measure of professional approval for an "enlightened" decision.

At the beginning of the case, the social worker acted to help the involved professional colleagues accept the right of the couple to self-determination. At the same time, she provided help and guidance in placing the infant in a foster home. In addition to making a referral to the appropriate agency, she acted as a consultant to the agency's worker on the special needs of an infant with Down syndrome. Despite the Carlins' initially strong resistance to counseling, the social worker succeeded in engaging them in an initial examination of their feelings about the birth of the child and the placement decision. Mrs. Carlin acknowledged problems with depression, anxiety, and sleeplessness. Although the case was terminated after only a short period of time when the family moved away for professional reasons, the Carlins were agreeable to counseling in their new community and accepted the referral made to a social worker in that area.

The social worker in the preceding case had identified her professional tasks as:

1. to help the clients engage in constructive examination of their dilemma;
2. to help other professionals involved in the case to modify their negative attitudes;
3. to advocate on behalf of the family their right to self-determination;
4. to connect the family with the appropriate community resources; and
5. to protect the best interests of the child throughout the placement process.

Thus, the intervention included counseling, consultation, collaboration, and linkage services.

Evaluation of the outcomes of the helping process are necessary not only for professional accountability but also for providing tentative predictions of future progress and helping needs. As shown in Chapter 4, genetic disorders frequently are chronic in nature. Also, we have identified that the presence of a genetic defect assumes importance in relation to developmental life stages. This implies that in evaluating the help given, the outcomes need to be assessed in terms of their compatibility with changing goals and realities. Perhaps most importantly, the help provided and the desired outcomes should be directed toward providing a basis for enabling clients to acquire greater competencies in coping with their genetic disorder over time.

A viable framework for clinical social work practice in genetics emerges when the governing principles of general clinical practice are linked to the characteristic features of genetic disorders and the range of social needs evoked by the impact and presence of genetic conditions. These are set within the context of a unitary practice approach focused on persons-in-situations and directed toward the enhancement of psychosocial functioning.

THE SOCIAL WORKER IN THE CLINICAL GENETICS SETTING

Discussion throughout this volume emphasizes the contributions to genetic services of social workers in a wide range of practice settings. The formal genetics clinic is only one point along a continuum of services that often are called for before and after formal genetic evaluations and counseling. Social workers also have a particular contribution to make as members of specialized genetic counseling teams. The broad definition of genetic counseling, cited in Chapter 2, of the American Society of Human Genetics (Fraser, 1974) suggests the use of an interdisciplinary approach. It includes as basic elements of genetic counseling efforts to help counselees understand their options, make appropriate choices, and adjust to their situation.

Currently only a relatively small number of social workers are employed in genetics programs. This may result in part from the lack of adequate funding of genetics services, the continuing use of models of genetic counseling that give low priority to psychosocial concerns, or a perceived lack of adequate training of social workers to assume these positions. However, any efforts to increase social work's direct participation in genetic counseling will demand clear delineation of the specific contributions that social workers can make on the genetics team. Table 9 suggests one approach to defining these functions in areas of clinic referral, diagnosis, medical management, and adjustment to the disorder, as well as in teaching, research, consultation, and program development.

In keeping with the practice principles outlined in the first section of this chapter, the social work role outlined in Table 9 parallels accepted definitions of clinical social work in medical settings. The differences emerge solely in the focus on the genetic context of the medical situation. Many of the functions described in Table 9 also overlap with the contributions that are made by social workers involved with genetics clients in settings outside the genetic counseling service.

TABLE 9

Roles of Clinical Geneticist and Social Worker in Genetic Counseling[*]

Clinical Geneticist	Social Worker
Clinic Referral	
screening, suitability for clinic	preparation of clients for genetic clinic: clarifying expectations of/for clients, explaining clinic procedures
Diagnosis	
physical exam, work-up interpretation of clinical findings	obtaining social history and data on current social situation gathering pedigree information, pulling together information resources: family bible, baby book, pictures, etc. assessment of potential impact of diagnosis on client and family
Medical Management	
treatment follow-up supervision counseling on medical concerns provision of genetic information	interpretation/clarification of medical/genetic information counseling on psychosocial issues related to medical management, barriers to following needed treatment regimens provision of help for concrete needs related to medical management: finances, babysitting, in-home health aids, transportation, etc. linkage to community services

[*]Based on current definition of genetic counseling (Fraser, 1974) and the use of an interdisciplinary collaborative approach.

TABLE 9 (continued)

Adjustment to Genetic Disorder

counseling on reproductive risks
medical interventions as needed:
  prenatal diagnosis,
  screening of newborn and extended
  family members at risk, review and
  updating of genetic information, etc.
provision of emotional support
ongoing counseling for medical questions as needed

counseling on nonmedical issues such
  as special schooling
counseling for psychosocial impact on
  affected individuals and family, includes marital, family, parental relationships and problems in
  living generated by genetic disorders
provision of emotional support
help with decision-making dilemmas
referral to and coordination with needed
  community resources
liaison between clients and medical staff
work with significant others and systems in the client's environment
developing and leading support groups
  for affected individuals and family
  members

Other

community education
program development
consultation
research

community education
program development
consultation
research

ISSUES IN ASSESSMENT

The particular role of clinical social work within the mission of the social work profession, is thought to be represented by the ability to conduct a bio-psycho-social assessment of persons-in-situations and to conduct or facilitate interventions based on these assessments. (Ewalt, 1980, p. 23)

The Genetic-Social Assessment

Over 20 years ago, Harriet Bartlett recognized that defining a medical-social problem is a difficult intellectual and social process. To those unfamiliar with the health field, it might seem that all any social worker without experience in the medical setting needs to gain is some additional knowledge about disease and health care and add this to the body of social work knowledge. "However, the process is not of adding one and one to make two, but of identifying social interactions in a constellation of organic, psychic, social, and cultural factors" (Bartlett, 1961, p. 175). Bartlett's conceptualization, which appears to best describe social work practice in the health field, is that of the person or group in a social situation in which the medical problem represents the central concern. If one substitutes a genetic problem for a medical problem, we can easily see that this is how we have previously characterized clinical practice. Within this frame of reference, the social worker is called upon to assess the medical, social, and emotional aspects and to integrate these elements of the genetic social situation in considering the nature of the interventions to be used. The following case illustration reflects this process:

> The client was a 40-year-old man with a severe dwarfing syndrome. When first seen, he was hospitalized because of severe respiratory problems as well as skeletal deformities. His elderly mother was referred to the social worker because of her indecision about giving permission for orthopedic surgery, which would allow her son to be more comfortable for the remaining years of his life. Because the patient had a severe hearing impairment, he had not been directly addressed by the medical staff. One of the first steps taken by the social worker was to enable the patient to wear his hearing aid and involve him directly in the counseling session. In considering possible areas to explore with the patient, the social worker reflected on her knowledge that individuals with genetic defects may blame their parents for passing on the defective gene. On the other hand, they may feel they are causing parental or family conflict. Genetically affected individuals may believe that part of their being is bad, and therefore they are worthless people. They may become extremely dependent on their parents and let them make all decisions, afraid to assert their own rights or form their own opinions.

> Once the patient was directly engaged, it was learned that he felt he owed it to his parents to accede to their wishes and did not feel worthy of deciding for himself even such a critical decision as his own surgery. With brief support, the patient was able to reveal the shame he felt for having caused his parents such trouble by having this terrible genetic disease. Ironically, his mother was greatly relieved when the social worker encouraged the patient to exert his right to make his own decision. The patient was pleased to be dealt with directly by the medical staff and to be recognized as a competent adult, in spite of his genetic disorder and tiny size.

The case demonstrates how the social worker is required to use basic knowledge of human behavior and of the psychosocial impact of genetic disorders to assess adequately the nature of the genetic-social situation and the ability of the client to take and to use help. The interrelatedness of the genetic components to life events, to personality development, and to psychosocial functioning is illustrated further in the following case:

A 13-year-old boy with Marfan syndrome* was severely trauma-
tized by the deaths of his mother and favorite brother, both of whom
had also had Marfan syndrome. On referral for genetic diagnosis,
he was noted to be depressed and displaying little affect. When encouraged to talk about his reaction to the genetic diagnosis, he
revealed a low self-esteem. He believed no one liked him because he
was so tall and skinny. The favorite people in his life had deserted
him by dying; his peers at school laughed at his physical difference;
and his father did not want him to come to live with him. The social
worker helped this adolescent boy to realize that he was not to blame
for the death of his mother and brother and to voice his apprehension about early death for himself. In addition, the social worker
was able to work out living arrangements with his maternal aunt and
to effect periodic visits with his father who was remarried and had a
new family.

With the boy's agreement, a referral was made to a social worker in
his aunt's community so that he could continue to work on his feelings of low self-esteem and receive support as he adjusted to his new
home and school.

Bartlett's (1961) model of constant elements in assessment of a
medical-social situation (p. 179) provides a guide for assessment of a
genetic social situation. The following elements, viewed separately and in
interaction, require careful and systematic exploration:

1. *The genetic situation.* The genetic problem includes the diagnosis,
   the method of transmission (if known), the physical illness and
   disabilities attached to the disorder, the prognosis and the trajectory
   of the disorder, and the implications for psychosocial functioning.
2. *The client* (individual and/or family). A psychodynamic assessment
   of client functioning—biologically; socially; psychologically, including appraisal of motivation, adaptive capacities, strengths and
   patterns, social roles and functioning.
3. *Environment.* Assessment of transactions with the environment including strengths and problems therein, family functioning as affected by and as affecting client functioning, other social relationships, socioeconomic and cultural aspects impinging on the client's
   situation, and nature of resources in the community.
4. *The client's feelings about these elements.*
5. *The client-worker relationship,* which determines where the client
   wishes to begin, the accessibility of the client to use and take help,
   and provides the context in which the helping is effected.

Any of these elements, separately or in combination, may dominate in a particular situation. Although these elements are found in the general social work practice literature, it is the distinctive constellation of elements and the subtle interplay of the genetic-social problem with other elements that mark the focus of the genetic-social situational assessment.

The Use of the Pedigree

There is one tool that can be used in the assessment process that is singularly different in clinical practice with genetic concerns—the pedigree. The pedigree is a method of recording essential family history of genetic defects and of documenting patterns of inheritance and familial disorders (see Chapter 3).[1] The social worker employed outside specialized genetic settings may wish to gather pedigree data as a basis for referral when a client brings a concern that seems to imply genetic involvement. Although the genetic counselor will repeat some of this process in developing a more detailed pedigree, the time spent with the referring social worker in developing a preliminary family tree serves at least two important purposes. First, this background information provides early assistance to the genetic counselor in arriving at an accurate diagnosis. The social worker who already knows and is trusted by the client may find it easier to obtain sensitive details about family members who have been rejected or stigmatized because of their physical disorder. In the process of developing a family pedigree it also may become evident that distant relatives must be contacted to obtain additional information, photographs, or medical records. Since diagnosis may be delayed until such information is obtained, the referring social worker who has developed a preliminary pedigree can work in collaboration with the genetic counselor to assist the client in obtaining this information. A second benefit is the opportunity it provides to acquaint clients with the process they will encounter during the genetic evaluation and counseling. The social worker can point out that their review of the family tree is actually the first stage of the genetic evaluation and highlight the kinds of questions the clients might anticipate when they see the genetic counselor.

Often the worker can combine collection of relevant genetic and social data and thus to some extent merge the processes of assessment and of taking the individual and/or family's physical history. It is not unusual to obtain an illuminating picture of the depth of family relationships when sketching out the family tree—who is close to whom; who is alienated from whom; where people live, far or near, and who is available as a support system; who is the family historian; what is disturbing the family; etc. For purposes of referral, precision of pedigrees drawn by genetics professionals is not required. The social worker can take the pedigree and develop a rough sketch of the family tree simply by learning and using the basic universal pedigree symbols (see Figures 5 and 6 and Chapter 3).

A case in point can be seen in the use of the pedigree in the S. family:

> While taking the pedigree, the social worker learned that all of the mentally retarded members were on the mother's side and that these individuals were all male, including Mrs. S.'s father, her two sons, various children of her sisters, and several first cousins. One affected cousin, age 54, lived with his elderly mother in an area close by, and this family unit was closely involved with the S. family. Mrs. S.'s aunt took on the grandmother role to the S. children and was their protector, adviser, and supporter, especially for Mrs. S. The aunt was instrumental in providing the family history for individuals going clear back to 1850. The genetic diagnosis—made solely on pedigree data—was of mental retardation which was sex-linked genetically; that is, an error on the X chromosome, resulting in affected males.

> The social worker also learned that the aunt had concerns about what would happen to her son should she die. Referral was made to the Regional Center, which coordinated services for the mentally retarded. The Center not only helped the aunt to arrange for conservatorship for the son but also arranged for him to become involved in an adult activity program for the first time in his life. Additionally, the aunt proved to be an ally in helping the S. parents to resolve their dilemma about the reproductive risks and to arrange sterilization for their mildly retarded 18-year-old son.

Genetic pedigrees also contribute to research efforts to identify individuals or families affected or at risk for certain genetic disorders (Krush, 1981). Initial pedigree data help to determine:

> which branches of the family need not be called in for examination because they are not at risk, which members are at risk and should be pursued with vigor, and which members need not be asked to come for examination until it is known they are definitely at risk. (p. 41)

In such investigations, the social worker not only seeks the cooperation of immediate family members but also attempts to enlist their help in finding other potentially affected kindred.

Thus the persons involved in such genetic studies usually are not seeking help with a medical problem. In fact, they may not have the condition under study, or, prior to the interview with the social worker, they may not have been aware of its presence in themselves or in their family. Particularly in cases in which early diagnosis offers significant hope of treatment and prevention of more serious problems, the social worker and other members of the genetics research team are likely to feel considerable urgency in reaching members of extended families. As Krush (1981) points out, however, the social work outreach efforts must include both ethics and tact in order to prevent initially negative reactions and refusals to participate.

It is also important to note that in addition to expectable scientific and medical benefits to family and community, the gathering of pedigree data in family research studies can yield indirect benefits for families: "compilation of family genealogies for distribution to family members; opportunity to meet distant relatives about which one had no previous knowledge; and knowledge of the history and culture of a distant country from which one's ancestors emigrated" (Krush, 1981, p. 47).

Decision Making and Risk Taking[2]

The issues evoked in pursuing risky behaviors and making decisions in the face of uncertainties are of special significance in the genetics field because of its frequent focus on reproductive risks and prenatal diagnosis. In assessing risk-taking behavior, what the social worker is basically trying to do is evaluate the nature of the client's decision making. The many factors that induce flaws and biases in processing information and making use of probabilistic data have been noted in Chapter 4. These factors should be incorporated into assessment with clients who are making decisions in the face of the uncertainties often generated by genetic information. Caution should be used when attempting even the most tentative estimate about the "correctness" of a client's final choice. The extensive literature on decision making does indicate, however, that the "quality of the procedures" used by the decision maker in selecting a course of action influences the likelihood of reaching a decision that is best for that individual in the long run. Janis and Mann (1977, p. 11) have summarized seven major activities that research evidence indicates characterize the most effective decision-making procedures:

The decision maker, to the best of his/her ability and within his/her information-processing capabilities,

1. thoroughly canvasses a wide range of alternative courses of action;
2. surveys the full range of objectives to be fulfilled and the values implicated by the choice;
3. carefully weighs whatever he/she knows about the costs and risks of negative consequences, as well as the positive consequences, that could flow from each alternative;
4. intensively searches for new information relevant to further evaluation of the alternatives;

5. correctly assimilates and takes account of any new information or expert judgment to which he/she is exposed, even when the information or judgment does not support the course of action he/she initially prefers;
6. reexamines the positive and negative consequences of all known alternatives, including those originally regarded as unacceptable, before making a final choice;
7. makes detailed provisions for implementing or executing the chosen course of action, with special attention to contingency plans that might be required if various known risks were to materialize.

These seven characteristics provide a beginning framework for the social worker in assessing whether a client is engaging in thoughtful decision making. Clients who engage in these activities are not more likely to reach a "rational" decision or even necessarily one with which the social worker will agree, but their orientation in arriving at a choice can be characterized as one of "vigilant information processing" (Black, 1981). As Janis and Mann (1977) conclude,

Especially for complex choices involving multiple objectives, we expect that a moderate or high degree of vigilant information processing is a necessary, albeit insufficient, condition for arriving at a decision that will prove satisfactory to the decision-maker in the long run. (p. 12)

Black (1981) has suggested adapting the "decisional balance sheet" approach for use in genetic decision making. This tool was designed to assist people in developing a vigilant information-processing style in their decision making. The social worker can ask the client to classify all the pro and con considerations involved in a given decision into the four categories described below.

1. Utilitarian gains and losses for self. This category includes all expected effects of the decision with regard to personal, utilitarian objectives. For example, the couple who has had one mentally retarded child must consider such issues as the financial costs of the second child, the drain on emotional and physical energies, and the loss of time from work and social activities.

2. Utilitarian gains and losses for significant others. Considerations in this category pertain to the goals and needs of persons in one's social network, particularly family. Parents must consider the likely impact of another child, whether normal or defective, on the family system. Other siblings may be deprived of privacy, face added economic constraints, and have to manage with less of their parents' time. On the other hand, parents also must consider the beneficial aspects of providing a sibling for a previous offspring.

3. *Self-approval or disapproval.* The client must consider those internalized moral standards, ego ideals, and components of self-image that are critical aspects of any important decision. Essentially these are matters of self-esteem. Among the questions a person should weigh are: "Will I feel proud or ashamed of myself if I make this choice? Will I be living up to my ideal? Will this decision enable me to become the kind of person I want to be?" (Janis & Mann, 1977, p. 139).

4. *Approval or disapproval by others.* The question here becomes "Will my friends and loved ones feel that I made the right choice?" The possibilities and likely impact of negative social feedback, including criticism and ridicule, must not be ignored since the approval or disapproval of reference groups and reference persons can be a powerful source of post-decisional regret (Janis & Mann, 1977). Unanticipated disapproval from close friends and relatives may even at times precipitate hasty reversals of earlier decisions. Attitudes toward further reproduction in the face of genetic risks vary widely, with the decision of whether to terminate a pregnancy following prenatal testing engendering particularly strong reactions both for and against the choice. As indicated in the study by Lippman-Hand and Fraser (1979a), counselees frequently sought some sort of cues as to "appropriate," i.e., acceptable, behaviors. It would appear that, at least for some time to come, the socially ambiguous nature of the choices raised by genetic issues will make it especially difficult but important for clients to evaluate carefully the reactions of others.

By using this information as a starting point, the client can begin to explore possible sources of difficulty in maintaining the decision as well as likely causes of postdecisional regret. One aim in assessing the decision-making process used by clients is to predict vulnerability to subsequent setbacks by identifying the main sources of conflict (Janis & Mann, 1977). This leads us to the larger question of the social worker's responsibility to identify who is at increased psychosocial risk in the genetic situation. Risk factors in relation to decision making will be considered first, followed by discussion of other factors that can contribute to increased vulnerability in psychosocial functioning.

Screening for Difficulties in Decision Making

As has been noted throughout our discussions, clients with genetic problems are confronted with the need to make decisions about complex, emotionally laden issues. We can reasonably conclude that clients who have deficient decision-making patterns also are those who may well fall into the class of psychosocial high-risk clients. It is important therefore for social workers to be able to make adequate assessments of whether clients are at increased risk for deficiencies in their decision-making procedures. Initial guidelines to assist the social worker in making this assessment have been specified by Janis and Mann (1977). They have identified four conditions in their decision-making model, which they consider prerequisites for a pattern of vigilant information processing. These conditions are considered along with their implications for genetic decision making.

1. Awareness of serious threat if no protective action is taken (i.e., low confidence in the prior course of action or inaction). For example, a person facing a genetic risk for future offspring first must experience some concern about the possible consequences if no efforts are made to avoid pregnancy. A moderate degree of stress is needed before an individual becomes aroused sufficiently to give careful consideration to alternatives and their consequences. The implications of this issue can be seen in those cases in which the genetic disorder has marked variation in the severity of its expression. A parent who has experienced no serious problems as a result of having the disorder or seeing it in another offspring may not become fully aware that in fact the risks are quite high and that the next child could just as easily have a severe, debilitating expression of the disorder.

2. Awareness of serious risks if the most salient protective action is taken (i.e., low confidence in whatever new course of action is being considered). Following genetic counseling parents may quickly conclude that future pregnancies must be prevented without full awareness of the possible interpersonal and psychological risks that may be involved in such a choice. In other words, the most obvious alternative course may not necessarily be a good choice for them, yet they are unable to undertake a vigilant consideration of alternatives unless they are aware that negative consequences may follow.

3. Moderate or high degree of hope that a search for information and advice will lead to a better (less risky) escape route (i.e., high confidence that a satisfactory solution exists and can be discovered). Individuals facing genetic risks in fact may have few escape routes open to them and see only two options: forego pregnancy or face the risk of bearing a defective child. A vigilant consideration of the alternatives will not increase the options, but if couples do not engage in such a process they run the risk of finding themselves unprepared for the consequences of any decision they make.

4. Belief that there is sufficient time to search and deliberate before a serious threat will materialize (i.e., high confidence that the yet undiscovered, satisfactory solution can be found within the time available). Unfortunately many parents faced with genetic risks have only limited time for decision making. For some, discovery of a biochemical or chromosome defect during prenatal testing comes at a stage in the pregnancy when there is only a brief time left for a legal abortion. Others may feel the press of the biological clock as they grow older and have less and less time for childbearing.

Review of the prerequisites for vigilant information processing indicates that people facing genetic issues are likely to be at high risk for deficiencies in decision making. Decisions may be made precipitously out of concern about time limitations and without careful consideration of their long-term, personal implications. Patterns of "defensive avoidance" may emerge involving selective inattention to or forgetting of certain facts, distortions of the meanings of warning messages, construction of wishful rationalizations that minimize negative consequences, or attempts to turn over responsibility for the decision to medical professionals, spouses, or other family members (Janis & Mann, 1977).

The specific characteristics of vigilant information processing and the decisional balance sheet approach are offered as suggestions for social work practice and research. The ultimate usefulness of these frameworks for social work practice remains to be proven through systematic investigation. Heuristically, they appear to hold much promise for helping to identify particularly vulnerable clients through assessment of their decision-making procedures, identification of any deficiencies in these procedures, and clarification of the sources of any anxieties or ambivalence.

Identification of Psychosocial Risk Factors

It is incumbent on social workers to identify vulnerable clients and, if possible, provide interventions to prevent the development or exacerbation of psychosocial problems. Who are the psychosocially high-risk clients in the genetic situation? How can we assess who is most likely to be in trouble in coping with the crisis of a genetic diagnosis? Critical factors arising in the specific area of decision making have been considered in the previous section. Clinical experience and beginning objective studies of psychological reactions to genetic counseling and prenatal diagnostic procedures (M. A. Antley, R. M. Antley, & Hartlage, 1973; R. M. Antley, 1976; R. M. Antley, Hartlage, & Kopetzke, 1972; Ashery, 1977; Beeson & Golbus, 1979; Fraser & Levy, 1972) leads us to believe that there are a number of other factors that singly or in combination lead to high-risk status. Ashery (1977), for instance, identified that approximately 10–15% of the population undergoing amniocentesis would need some level of emotional support from clinic staff. Two variables in particular were isolated by Ashery (1977) as indicative of a situation meriting social work involvement: (a) extreme anxiety, and (b) a positive diagnosis of a genetic problem in the fetus. Beeson and Golbus (1979), in their study of anxiety engendered by amniocentesis, found that those at higher psychological risk for anxiety included cases in which the following factors were present: (a) previous child with a chromosomal disorder, (b) history of repeated miscarriage, (c) spotting in the pregnancy, (d) poor health history of the mother, and (e) primagravity.

Rice and Doherty (1982), in a recent study of consumers' views on prenatal diagnosis, identified that couples appear to experience the most significant stresses while considering the possibility of abortion and while awaiting the test results. Even more stress was reported if the couple had not made a decision about abortion prior to the test or when there was ambivalence or opposition to abortion because of religious principles. Also of interest was the finding of a correlation between the frequency of church attendance and the men's answers to questions about abortion. No such correlation was found with the responses of the women. Rice and Doherty recommend the inclusion of certain screening questions for initial interviews. The information provided would help to identify high-risk individuals and also indicate a need for social work intervention either during the test process or following detection of a fetal defect. "Examples of important data would be: religious denomination, frequency of church attendance or other indicators of strength of religious affiliation, attitudes and ethical values toward abortion, and the concerns the couple have about the test" (Rice & Doherty, 1982, p. 55).

Table 10 provides a summary listing of factors to consider in the assessment of clients with genetic concerns. Variables listed in Table 10 encompass a wide range of factors typically considered in the general person-situation assessment. Placed within the context of the genetic event, they assume specific relevance and significance.

ISSUES IN INTERVENTION

The critical question for clinical practice is to ask how the social worker can intervene to help clients most effectively with their current challenges, to prepare for the future, and to strengthen their resources and capacities for coping. There is no way for the social worker to "fix" the genetic problem, but there are ways to help people to manage painful realities and to maximize the quality of their lives. The question can be raised as to what, if anything, is unique in intervening with clients who have genetic concerns. Are there special methods for helping these clients? Fundamentally, the modes, strategies, and principles of intervention are the same in genetics as in other domains of clinical social work practice. We have, however, stressed the attention to be paid to the genetic-social problem and its dynamic influences on the lives of clients. It follows that interventions will be determined and shaped by the unique

TABLE 10

Factors in the Assessment of Clients With Genetic Concerns

FACTOR	AREAS FOR EXPLORATION
Genetic Disorder	1. Implications for health status and physical functioning 2. Burden of care
Genetic Transmission	1. One or both parents implicated? 2. Other family members at risk? 3. Size and nature of recurrence risks?
Reproductive History	1. Childbearing experiences (miscarriages, abortions, stillbirths, pregnancies, etc.) 2. Previously affected children 3. Birth order of affected children 4. Primagravity 5. Reproductive aspirations - family planning
Psychosocial Situation 1. Family/social context	1. Demographic data (sex, marital status, ages, family size, household members, education, employment, income, religion, race/ethnicity, etc.) 2. Interpersonal relationships: marital, parent-child, family, significant others 3. Social problems/assets: financial, school, employment, etc. 4. Current health status of family: physical and emotional resources 5. Family history of genetic diseases, birth defects, other health disorders or anomalies 6. External resources: support systems, significant reference groups (e.g., church, fraternal organization)
2. Psychological context	1. Attitudes towards illness, disability, abortion, deviance, medical care, health professionals, genetic interventions, etc. 2. Nature and intensity of religious beliefs 3. Perceptions of genetic problem 4. Meanings given to genetic event 5. Emotional-mental health status 6. Patterns of coping, stress management 7. Decision-making patterns

configuration of elements comprising the genetic-social-situational assessment. We have also highlighted the fact that many new dilemmas are
emerging relative to genetic disorders; dilemmas which lack tried and
true benchmarks for intervention. This leads frequently to uncertainty
about practice strategies in certain genetic situations. As one social
worker has observed, "I am following a population of patients with
degenerative [genetic] diseases. I have . . . been faced with many
clinical quandaries for which there has been little guidance in the literature" (Goldring, personal communication, 1982). Particular issues in
intervention in the genetics area that we will consider in the following sections include: (a) sharing of genetic information; (b) confusion due to
genetic complexities; (c) value conflicts; (d) alternative health beliefs; (e)
development of support groups; and (f) referrals to genetic counseling.
These areas have a distinctive specificity related to the current state of
genetic knowledge and technology and to the perplexing demands and
questions confronting clients who have genetic disorders. Social workers
are likely to confront these practice issues in the course of helping clients
with their genetic concerns and dilemmas.

Sharing of Genetic Information

Dilemmas frequently emerge about the proper procedures for sharing
of genetic information. At issue are the limits on responsibility for in-
forming close family members or distant relatives that they have or may
have hereditary disorders. A number of questions are raised: (a) to whom
does this information belong; (b) is informed consent by the primary
client prerequisite to sharing this genetic information with others; (c) who
should do the telling—the client, the doctor, the social worker, etc; (d)
under what conditions, if any, should the information be withheld; and (e)
under what conditions should the information be given. The following
case illustrates some of the dilemmas connected with such sharing of
genetic information:

The P. family is middle class; the father works as an electrician and
the mother is a housewife. There are three children: David, 14,
Mark, 11 (the patient), and Lisa, 8. Mark was diagnosed as having
ALD (adrenoleukodystrophy*) at age 9 when he began to show de-
clining motor and cognitive abilities. Lisa has been healthy in all re-
spects. David has had normal development except for a minor learning disability. The family has been seen at the clinic a number of
times, and many of the issues discussed with the social worker were
typical of any family with a handicapped child. For example, there
was marital conflict over the issue of discipline versus leniency;
also, the youngest daughter had some personal problems because of

lack of equal attention from her parents. In addition, dilemmas about information sharing also arose because of the specific nature of this rare, genetic disorder.

The primary issue involved a particular set of genetic counseling dilemmas. Since there was a possibility that the older brother, David, also might have the disease, the staff wondered: (1) whether they should routinely test nonsymptomatic male siblings such as David; (2) when and how they should approach the parents if they decided to offer such a test; and (3) what they should do with the results if positive, i.e., should they share this information with the child and, if so, who should tell him?

The ramifying issues in the above case are sensitive and serious. In such dilemmas about information sharing, the social worker seeks a clear understanding of what the client knows and what the client wants to know. The worker must be mindful of the possible effects of the information giving or information withholding, as well as the client's capacities for coping with stress and change. Certainly, when distant relatives are implicated and such determinations may be impossible to make, the social worker's focus may shift to assisting the affected client and/or immediate family in making similar assessments of the needs and interests of genetically implicated relatives. In addition, legal and ethical constraints and protections of clients' rights to confidentiality and privacy cannot be overlooked. As always, there is the relevance of the ongoing genetic-social assessment.

Confusion Due to Genetic Complexities

In Chapter 4 we identified that genetic problems are characterized by complexity. Many clients struggle with understanding the physiological facts about their genetic defects, the nature of genetic transmission, and the probabilistic risks of reproductive recurrence. An issue in practice relates to how to help clients to achieve a clearer comprehension of their genetic information. One way of helping is to provide the opportunities for clients to discuss freely what they do and do not understand. This requires help by the worker in facilitating the educational process at the client's own learning pace. It goes almost without saying, perhaps, that it is incumbent on social workers to have clarity themselves about the relevant genetic knowledge, otherwise there is high risk for compounding the confusion of the client.

The all too frequent situations of scientific uncertainty associated with genetic diagnoses may make it particularly difficult to address the presenting psychosocial concerns of the client.

The M. case involves a family with a newly identified disorder that geneticists believe follows an autosomal dominant inheritance pattern with wide variability in severity of expression. There are three affected children, ages: 9 months, 2 years, and 3-1/2 years. The mother is again pregnant; there is no prenatal test for the disorder. The affected children are all facially disfigured ("look terrible!" is how they have been described), are mildly delayed in mental development, and require speech therapy. Two of the children already have had surgery for premature closure of skull sutures and one child has had cosmetic surgery on the cheek bones.

Although the father in this family is believed to be the carrier of this autosomal dominant gene, considerable uncertainty remains. There is a possibility that the mother may also express the disorder. This raises the questions of whether this is a rare problem of two carriers of the same dominant disorder, in which case, the recurrence risk jumps from 50% to 75%, or if there are two similar disorders implicated. The presenting problems raised by the mother related to whether or not she also had the disorder and if her recurrence risk was higher in her current pregnancy.

This is an intact, stable family who are observant Mormons. They are opposed to abortion and the use of contraceptives.

Mrs. M. will need assistance in order to understand that, given the current state of knowledge and technology, no way yet exists to determine with certainty whether or not she also has the disorder. Also, it will be important for her to understand that the risks of recurrence remain relatively high whether or not she herself is affected. If these salient data are clearly communicated, Mrs. M. may then be able to focus on the implications for herself and her family should this new offspring be similarly affected. It would be hoped that clarification of the facts might also allow Mrs. M. to address other possible underlying concerns or anxieties that she may have about the current pregnancy.

Sometimes confusion about the genetic data results in distortions that affect emotions and behaviors. The following case example (Plumridge, personal communication, 1982) shows how clarification of the genetic data and the meanings attached to this information paved the way for a group of mothers to free their energies for work on other issues involved in living with seriously handicapped children. The group was comprised of women identified as carriers of balanced chromosomal translocations. Each had borne a child with serious disabilities that resulted from inheriting that translocation in an unbalanced state.

The initial group session began with the question: "What is the difference in having a severely handicapped child due to a chromosomal abnormality than one that is born with severe defects due to other, nongenetic causes?'' The following content emerged out of this session:

1. The mothers noted a sense of relief in having a precise diagnosis, no matter how catastrophic. In the case of chromosomal translocations, the defect is actually visible under a microscope or enlarged for a karyotype.
2. Their sense of guilt was alleviated by the knowledge of the chromosome error. There were many things for which the mothers felt responsible but their, or their child's, previously unknown genetic makeup need not be one of these. It was what the mothers did with the knowledge of the genetic defect that was their responsibility.
3. The mothers experienced regret as carriers of a chromosome defect, yet having other family members also affected helped to remove the sense of isolation the diagnosis engendered.
4. The mothers felt a sense of responsibility toward their unborn children, and none wished another similarly affected child. They felt they could not undertake another pregnancy unless they had the emotional stamina to undergo an abortion, if this proved necessary. They were very aware of their individual recurrence risks, which ranged from 5 to 20% and the group spent a great deal of time on the topic of prenatal diagnosis.
5. The mothers had a need to involve intimately other family members for testing and counseling. They all learned quickly to analyze their individual family pedigrees to determine other family members at risk, although difficulties arose quite often when they actually attempted to educate the extended family about this highly technical and seemingly esoteric genetic information.

The remainder of the group sessions centered on the same issues any family faces in raising a severely handicapped child. The usual group process ensued, and the women gained a great deal of strength from each other. The worker concluded at the end of the sessions that many of the women felt more comfortable in planning another pregnancy and could verbalize their need for a normal child.

When the scientific data are unclear, clients may be particularly vulnerable to developing inappropriate self-blame and increased feelings of guilt. Sometimes these may be expressed in behaviors counterproductive to the health and well-being of the persons involved. In such situations intervention would be targeted to the alleviation or elimination of unrealistic or unfounded attitudes about responsibility. For instance, it is not uncommon for parents of genetically affected children to become overprotective and, in so doing, to create difficulties for their offspring. Parents of children with PKU,* for example, often experience difficulties in weaning their children off the bottle of Lofenalac, a special diet preparation (Harold, personal communication, 1982). Long delays in making the transition away from the bottle may seriously interfere with the children's normal developmental needs for increased textures and varieties of foods in their diets.

At other times, the parents' feelings about the genetic disorder and the complexity of the associated problems may interfere with their ability to communicate effectively basic facts about the disorder to the affected child and to assess adequately the accuracy of the child's understanding of that information. Distortions, confusion, and behavior problems may be the unfortunate result of parents' difficulties in communication. The following case situation illustrates how misunderstandings about the genetic defect created psychological difficulties for the affected child and problems in the parent-child relationship. It also shows how the worker's strategy for intervention included work with both parents and child, individually and as a family unit, offering emotional support, providing both personal and interpersonal counseling, and educating the clients about the relevant genetic information.

Jim, age 9, has PKU* and has been off the dietary treatment for 3 years. He is an average student who has always tested normally on IQ tests. His parents are well informed about the genetic disorder and believe they had given Jim all the appropriate information. When Jim was in the third grade, he became friends with a boy who was in the terminal phase of leukemia. After his friend's death, Jim developed temper tantrums and behavior problems. Upon recommendation by the school psychologists, Jim was taken to a child guidance clinic.

After 9 months of play therapy, Jim was able to discuss his PKU and revealed his worry that he had "a piece missing." Although his parents had given him information on PKU Jim had developed the distorted belief that a physical piece was missing from his body, a not unlikely distortion since in PKU there is a "missing" link in the metabolic chain that normally enables the body to metabolize phenylalanine. The goal in the helping endeavors was to reduce the anxiety of Jim and his parents by helping both child and parents to understand the child's fear about his own body and to clarify their knowledge about the disease. Through expressions of feelings and attaining of a more accurate cognitive conception of PKU, Jim was able to curb his acting-out behavior, and a better parent-child relationship evolved.

Clients often are given complicated genetic information at times when they are under considerable stress, e.g., after the birth of a child with serious defects or when contemplating further childbearing. As a result, clients often do not immediately think, much less ask, all of their questions. They do not always hear what is being said and, more often than not, will require time to digest and to consider the new information. Follow-up services with a social worker can be important in clarifying confusion and utilizing the genetic data to inform decision making. A social worker in a hemophilia program remarked,

> I do a great deal of genetic counseling. This is not a formal arrangement, but genetic questions for basic information and for help in decision making regarding family planning come up a great deal. Patients and family members don't want to go to a person they don't know. They want to get information and wrestle with this information with someone they know and trust. Genetic counseling is not a six session course. It is part of a patient's and family's lifetime quest to adjust to hemophilia. Different questions come up at different times. People need to hear the same information again and again. (Black, 1982)

Value Conflicts

A professional value conflict may become paramount in deciding on courses of action in working with genetic clients. For example, the worker may be confronted with the situation in which societal rights for promoting health and preventing defects collide with the personal rights of individuals for self-determination. The dilemma seen in the following case example concerned whether and how much influence should be exerted to persuade a client to have an abortion.

> Without a return to a restrictive diet low in phenylalanine women with PKU* are at extremely high risk of producing offspring with severe microcephaly (small heads) and mental retardation. Recently, an untreated mother with PKU (IQ 52) was referred to the clinic for genetic counseling and amniocentesis. She was 17 weeks pregnant and had not been following the restrictive diet necessary for reducing the risk to the fetus. Her first child is microcephalic and mentally retarded. The probability that this second child will be severely retarded was judged to be over 90%.

It is not always easy for the social worker to know how to deal with the question of future childbearing or termination of pregnancy. There is a fine line as to when this constitutes an invasion of privacy or when this is in the best interest of the person involved. The issue of personal biases of the worker comes to the forefront in such situations. Personal beliefs must neither be allowed to obscure professional values nor be imposed on clients. There needs to be open recognition of the differing moral and ethical views on controversial subjects such as abortion. The following further illustrates a number of the perplexing ethical issues that can arise in practice.

Rosa, a 17-year-old, single, Hispanic female, was referred by the Ob/Gyn resident for counseling regarding her first pregnancy, 11 weeks in gestation, and her genetic disease, osteogenesis imperfecta.* Rosa is in the 11th grade and lives with her parents and five siblings in a small, very overcrowded apartment. She receives aid through Social Security Disability. Rosa is dwarf-like, standing about 3 feet in height. She uses crutches and a wheel-chair and ambulates with difficulty. She has a long history of surgery for broken bones and bone displacements. Four years ago scoliosis was diagnosed.

This pregnancy was unplanned, and although Rosa did know about birth control, none had been used. The father, aged 21, wants nothing to do with Rosa or the baby. Rosa's parents are angry and extremely upset but supportive of good medical care. They are strongly opposed to abortion and in the past have picketed the pregnancy termination clinic at the hospital.

Rosa was seen in the prenatal clinic three times. In the last visit, Dr. B. explained to Rosa and her mother the risks, dangers, and alternatives pertaining to Rosa's pregnancy. The medical concerns are numerous. There is the possibility of problems with increased fractures and cardiac-pulmonary dysfunction due to her short stature and small trunk area. Labor and delivery would be a great challenge. There would be considerable risk to the fetus in the cramped environment afforded by Rosa's small body. In addition, because osteogenesis imperfecta is an autosomal dominant disorder, there would be a 50% chance that the offspring would inherit Rosa's disorder.

When seen by the social worker, Rosa had just received this information. Although she had not considered any of it before and said she would do some further thinking, she nevertheless firmly said that she planned to have the baby. She believed that abortion was "not right." Rosa had no plans for herself or the baby, although she did intend to drop out of school. Rosa was clearly angry but seemed unremorseful. The social worker's impression was that on a less-than-conscious level the pregnancy reflected unresolved feelings about her own handicaps and a desire to prove she could be "normal."

Although the medical staff in Rosa's case clearly favored termination of the pregnancy, her right to be self-determining remained as an important concern to be protected. There are those who would hold, however, that priority should go to the interests of society, since in the long run society pays for the care of the dependent and handicapped. Individuals who hold such beliefs might elect a more directive approach with Rosa, all but insisting that she have an abortion. The rights of the unborn child also require consideration. Does the child have a right to be born regardless of the risks or should priority go to protecting it from a hazardous birth and high genetic risks? There are no easy answers when important values collide.

The social worker has a professional responsibility to assist the client in reaching reasonable resolutions to such value conflicts. This requires active involvement by the client in values clarification and decision making. The issues must be examined in terms of the individual client's own values and beliefs with careful attention given to articulating the points of value conflict and the consequences of alternative actions. Open efforts to modify certain values or beliefs that appear harmful to a client may be in order at times. Throughout all such helping efforts, however, social workers must seek to clarify their own values and ethical principles in an effort to avoid inadvertently imposing them on their clients. When approached in this way, value conflicts can become a context for helping and an opportunity for fostering the client's growth and competency. A similar process can be employed by the social worker in order to help resolve value conflicts arising between professional colleagues, with the important restriction that collaborative professional decisions are bounded by what serves the best interests of clients and not by personal preferences.

Development of Support Groups

The confusing and stigmatizing nature of many genetic disorders may leave affected individuals and families feeling alone and different from others. Often they have never met another person with their rare disorder or even one similar to it. Support groups thus represent an important source of assistance for genetic clients, breaking down the sense of isolation and providing clients with an opportunity to affirm their competence by helping each other.

The group is an enterprise in mutual aid, an alliance of individuals who need each other, in varying degrees, to work on certain common problems. The important fact is that this is a helping system in which the clients need each other . . . . This need to use each other, to create not one but many helping relationships, is a vital ingredient of the group process and constitutes a common need. (Schwartz, 1961, p. 18)

The nature of genetic disorders often suggests a need for a variety of groups pertinent to a given disorder or set of related disorders. The basic question in developing any group service, what type of group is needed, is likely to have multiple answers. The importance of groups for affected individuals is perhaps self-evident, but as familial disorders, genetic diseases have an impact on a range of people. When the affected individual is a child, groups may be indicated for unaffected siblings, parents, and grandparents. The spouses, siblings, offspring, or caretakers of affected adults have particular concerns that may warrant separate groups. In all cases, the burden associated with the disorder and the pattern of genetic inheritance will influence not only the types of groups that will be needed but also the central issues of concern. For example, parents with offspring who have autosomal recessive disorders both have contributed an altered gene to the affected child and thus are likely to have a different experience than parents who may feel an unequal sense of responsibility in bearing a child with an autosomal dominant or X-linked disorder. The later age of onset of certain autosomal dominant disorders, such as Huntington disease, places particularly difficult stress on individuals who carry the 50-50 chance of developing the disorder during middle adulthood. As demonstrated in the following, the variability in severity of expression seen in many genetic disorders also must be considered for its impact on group composition. An important task for the social worker in planning a group thus is the careful assessment of the degree of homogeneity or heterogeneity across various dimensions that is likely to prove most useful in achieving the group's purposes.

The social worker and coleader of an ongoing group for affected adults with neurofibromatosis* observed that the formation of a subgroup appeared to be impeding the work of the group as a whole. They explored this problem with the group members and learned that several young, unmarried women, not obviously affected by the disease, had emerging concerns about sexuality and dating issues. They found it difficult to raise these concerns in the group because they felt uncomfortable and frightened by the severely affected, older members. Although they did not want to identify with these older members, they nevertheless feared that they might develop the same symptoms of the disease. The group leaders concluded that a separate group for young adults would be more beneficial for individuals like these mildly affected young women. This new group was formed and the original group was reconstituted to serve the older and more seriously affected members.

The social worker, recognizing the potential of groups for mutual aid, can choose among a range of options: (1) the initiation of a professionally led group, either time limited or open ended; (2) initiation of a self-help or mutual aid group in which the professional serves as a catalyst for and assists in the development of a group that ultimately will be led by the members themselves; and (3) referral to existing professionally led or self-help groups in the community.

Turning first to the issue of referral, we find an increasing number of support groups for individuals with genetic disorders. As indicated earlier in this chapter, social workers have demonstrated leadership in this area, and a growing literature by social work authors attests to their activity. The social worker wishing to refer a client to a professionally led group may find resources within specialty clinics of major medical centers or large voluntary associations organized around specific disorders. Clearinghouses also are springing up to provide referral information on the increasing number of self-help groups. At a recent national meeting (Weiss, 1983), one panel of speakers represented self-help groups serving affected individuals and families with sickle cell anemia, Marfan syndrome, osteogenesis imperfecta, Huntington disease, Tay-Sachs disease, and Down syndrome. For very rare conditions, a national or regional self-help network may be available to provide support and information to members by newsletters and telephone connections. One example is the recent development of a network for parents caring for children with trisomy 13 or 18. Although the majority of newborns with these chromosome disorders die shortly after birth, a small percentage may live one or more years. This unlikely burden of an already rare disorder necessitated ingenuity in linking parents in a national network of mutual aid.

The same stigma, sense of uniqueness, and rarity of genetic disorders that give groups so much potential for aid also can work against their formation or continuation. Affected individuals and families often do not know how to begin to locate others facing the same or similar problems. A personal sense of stigma or embarrassment may make them hesitant about coming together with others in a group, and they may not recognize how much they can gain from helping and being helped by their peers. Thus the social worker often must take the initiative in bringing genetic clients together.

The growing strength of the self-help movement (Gartner & Riessman, 1977; Katz & Bender, 1976; Lieberman & Borman, 1979; President's

Commission on Mental Health, 1978; Silverman, 1980; Silverman, MacKenzie, Pettipas, & Wilson, 1974; Tracy & Gussow, 1976) now challenges the professional to consider the merits of both professionally led and self-help groups in planning services. In our view, a focus on mutual aid as the primary goal of support groups prevents the polarization of these choices. Moreover, although the choices between initiating a professionally led or self-help group were presented as two separate options, social workers in practice find that such initially clear distinctions frequently become blurred.

As in the planning of any service, the social worker's decision to develop and lead a group should be based on careful assessment of the clients' needs. Morris and Hirsch (1982) have described the evolution of group services provided by social workers in the New York City Chapter of the National Huntington's Disease Association. They determined that the wide geographical spread of participants suggested the need for time-limited groups. The many members who had far to travel felt more willing to attend when they could make a clear commitment to a small number of sessions. Morris and Hirsch (1982) also noted the initially strong resistance to participation when groups were offered to primary caretakers of affected individuals and to those at-risk for developing Huntington disease. Potential members for both groups frequently remarked that they tried not to think about the disorder and could not see the benefit of getting together to talk about something they were actively trying to avoid. However, extensive outreach efforts by the social workers, requiring clarity in stating group purpose and brief time limits for commitment, were effective in engaging many of these individuals. Both groups in fact elected to continue beyond the initial contract of five sessions and meet monthly on an ongoing basis. This example highlights the importance of the professional's contribution in developing and leading groups when clients' ambivalence about group participation is high or the burden of their personal coping struggles has left them with little sense of how they might help or be helped by others with similar problems.

Even when professionally led groups are indicated as one facet of services, the creation of independent self-help groups will provide members with a unique opportunity for mutuality and reciprocity in sharing of experiences. Such groups emphasize the potential of members to take responsibility for helping each other without the direct guidance of a professional. Social workers can assist self-help groups in at least four ways: (1) by making referrals; (2) by serving on professional advisory boards; (3) by serving as consultants to existing groups; and (4) by initiating or helping to develop new groups (Silverman, 1978). Silverman (1980) has developed detailed guidelines for professional involvement in initiating self-help groups. If it is clear that there are potential resources in time and interest for attempting the start of such a group, the social worker from the outset can set a primary goal of "maximizing the capabilities of the members as helpers, to the point that they can take charge of the organization" (Silverman, 1980, p. 53). In many cases, however, self-help groups evolve out of professionally led groups. Miller (1976) described the process by which spouses of individuals with Huntington disease moved out from the initial counseling group led by the social worker to become an active, self-help group providing vital services to new families contacting the association. Schild (1964) reported on a group for parents of children with PKU. The initial group led by the social worker provided a vehicle for education and emotional support. Later, the group became self-sustaining and shifted its focus to social activities and political advocacy. Social workers initiating professionally led groups should assess early on the potentials for evolution into a self-help group and actively assist the members in developing the skills necessary to manage successfully their own organization. As the group achieves its autonomy, the social worker gradually shifts over to providing consultation, serving on the advisory board, and making referrals to the group.

National organizations for specific disorders exist as an important resource for self-help groups. Silverman (1980) argues that "the most effective way for a [self-help] group to sustain itself is to affiliate with a national organization from which it can receive direction and advice on programs and administration" (p. 12). Many such organizations have developed for genetic diseases. Examples include the National Marfan Foundation, Little People of America, National Huntington Disease Foundation of America, National Huntington's Disease Association, and Muscular Dystrophy Association.

The following describes the experiences of one social worker in developing a regional self-help network for parents of children with dwarfism (Weiss, personal communication, 1983). It illustrates the importance of working collaboratively with the national organization, Little People of America, in developing potential members and obtaining resources to enhance the development of the network. This example also provides an excellent illustration of the multiple and shifting roles of the social worker in leading and developing group services for clients with genetic concerns.

> In reviewing her caseload the social worker identified a need for average-sized parents with newly diagnosed dwarfed children to talk with other parents who had successfully adapted to having children with such difficulties. However, because of the rarity of these dwarfing conditions, she determined that it would be necessary to move out beyond the very small number of affected families in her own caseload. The social worker therefore contacted officials of the Little People of America (LPA) and obtained permission to conduct an

educational program for parents of dwarfed children in a seven-state region. Out of this program a parents' network evolved which was still, 2 years later, in operation.

At one point, the LPA provided these parents with legal assistance so that they could incorporate their group as "Parents of Dwarfed Children" (PDC). The two groups, LPA and PDC, have maintained a reciprocally supportive relationship, and PDC will be taken on under the umbrella of services available in the larger LPA program.

In the formative phases of the group, the social worker provided leadership in initiating the group and helping the members develop their goals and program. When the group achieved stability, cohesion, clarity of purpose, and its own leadership, the social worker relinquished her active role and became the consultant and resource person to the PDC.

Alternative Health Beliefs

Responses and reactions to genetic disease are shaped by the health beliefs held by people. Cultural traditions and beliefs influence notions people have about the causation and implications of familial health problems of birth defects. The dominant American culture demands a sense of obligation to do something about illness, to respect and accede to medical authority and knowledge, and to seek out and accept scientific data in order to understand the nature of our infirmities. Underlying these social obligations is the belief that sickness is a natural obstacle to be overcome. Such beliefs are not the dominant perspective of all people living in Western society, however.

Other cultural traditions often make different assumptions about health and illness that lead to different behaviors. For example:

Studies indicate that folk medical systems generally classify happenings, including physical diseases and mental conditions, as natural or supernatural (unnatural). Illness caused by natural sources are those in which a dangerous agent, such as cold air or impurities found in air, food, or water, enter the body to cause disease; bodily conditions or illnesses that are related to "God's will" may have been sent by God as punishment for sins or past transgressions.

[in certain Latin-American folk beliefs supernatural] or unnatural illnesses, sometimes referred to as an "artificial illness" are believed to be the result of an evil practiced by people. Examples include *el mal ojo* (the evil eye), *el mal puesto* (the evil put on), *mal de susto* (magical fright), *empacho* (swelling of the abdomen), and *caida de mollera* (fallen fontanelle). (Vespa, 1977, p. 86)[3]

Such beliefs run parallel to notions of a fix, a hex, or a mojo that are found in voodoo or witchcraft belief systems.

Persons whose behaviors are influenced by alternative health beliefs may find genetic information and counseling puzzling, confusing, or irrelevant to their way of life. This may pose problems when certain medical procedures are felt to be necessary or the cultural beliefs appear to be working against positive adaptation to the genetic situation. Knowledge of the health beliefs and traditions of the client's particular ethnic group and the extent to which these are held by the client is particularly important in identifying and attempting to bridge disparities that can arise in the process of communicating genetic information. Using the concept of "maternal impression," Vespa (1977) provides one example of the possible consequences that alternative health beliefs can have for understanding genetic principles.

> It is thought the mother's emotional state may affect the fetus. Feelings of pity, hate, or envy for another individual may cause the body to resemble that individual. A child may have Down syndrome because the mother saw another child so afflicted and felt pity. Likewise, a child may suffer seizures because the mother was having a seizure or was worrying about a relative who had this particular health disorder during her pregnancy. It is especially difficult for persons who believe that their transgressions are visited upon their children to accept that genetically determined disorders such as PKU or cystic fibrosis* occur by chance. (Vespa, 1977, p. 88)

The following illustrations highlight the importance of knowing the beliefs and attitudes held by other cultural groups about birth defects and inherited disease.[4]

> *Case One.* A young, Mexican couple came to the Birth Defects Evaluation Center with their 1-month-old baby girl, who had the typical clinical picture of Apert syndrome.* The diagnosis was confirmed in clinic. The clinical staff was not aware that the couple blamed the condition on a lunar eclipse which had taken place during the pregnancy. The acceptance of the eclipse as the causal agent implies that the woman is at fault. Guilt, either implied or direct, is assumed by the mother as it is her obligation to shield the fetus from the harmful rays of an eclipse by wearing one or several keys on her abdomen during the critical period. In contrast, the genetic data indicated that although either parent could carry the gene for Apert

(an autosomal dominant disorder) in an unexpressed form, the high rate of new mutations observed with this syndrome suggests that neither parent is likely to carry the gene. In this situation, the social worker chose to address directly the folk belief but in a nonjudgmental and nonthreatening way so as to help the couple hear and understand the scientific data. Reduction of the deep sense of guilt felt by the parents also was a primary goal, especially for the mother who was most directly implicated by the traditional beliefs.

Case Two. A young couple had their 4-year-old son diagnosed as having Schwartz-Jampel* syndrome. The parents appeared intelligent and seemed to understand the autosomal recessive gene transmission with its resulting one in four recurrence risk in each pregnancy. Alone with the social worker, however, the mother ventured the information that she had had a severe *susto* (fright) during her pregnancy. The fright related to the arrest and jailing of her husband and her lack of knowledge about his well-being or the outcome of the arrest. She believed the fright and anxiety may have infiltrated the fetus and caused the gene mutation. The worker pointed out how this belief in *susto* could result in guilt and self-blame. This freed the mother to examine with the worker the known scientific facts, which provided a different explanation for the child's disorder. Using a combination of support and education, and without directly challenging the folk belief or the woman's right to maintain her beliefs, the worker helped the mother to a personally more positive redefinition of the cause of her child's disorder.

This case also illustrates how the formal diagnostic, clinic sessions may be intimidating to clients from other ethnic and minority groups. Clients are likely to feel uncomfortable expressing different beliefs and understandings about genetic disease in front of authoritative professionals. Social workers practicing in genetics have found that people are most likely to discuss their cultural beliefs if a sense of rapport and trust is established between the worker and client. It has also been found beneficial to include in counseling grandparents and/or other significant others, who have influential ties with the family. They also often have relied on the folk beliefs to explain the birth defect or genetic problem and may prove to play an important role in either facilitating or blocking the family's integration of the Western medical perspectives into the traditions and beliefs of their ethnic group.

The influences of cultural mores and values on family life, marriage, and childbearing also need to be explored, as these may shape the ways in which genetic information, and particularly recurrence risks, will be received and utilized. Cultural traditions similarly may be involved in psychological reactions of clients. Thus, knowledge of traditional beliefs and values and the specific role they may play for a given client/family are necessary in order for the social worker to determine not only points for intervention but also the nature and style of interventive strategies.

Referrals to Genetic Counseling

A frequent question for social workers employed outside of genetics programs is when to make a referral for genetic counseling. Here there are some clear indications. Chapter 3 outlines many of the most common genetic disorders, available diagnostic procedures, and appropriate questions for a genetics clinic. Table 7 provides a detailed summary of the medical indications for referral. Certainly, referrals should be made when clients express concerns about inheritance or when the family history reveals the presence of familial patterns of severe illness and defects. Most important in making a referral to genetic counseling is clarity about the purpose of the referral. How will genetic counseling and information affect my clients and assist them in addressing their current concerns? As indicated in Table 7, a wide range of questions can appropriately be addressed to genetic counselors. Many clients seek genetic counseling for reasons other than learning about their own reproductive risks (Sorenson, et al., 1981). For example, many are seeking mainly a diagnosis or an understanding of the etiology of the abnormality that is affecting a child.

Unfortunately, situations involving possible referral do not always fall within these clear guidelines. Complex questions may arise which require careful assessment of a range of issues. The following case situation illustrates a worker's dilemma about making a referral for genetic counseling.

Roberto, age 14, was referred to the Pediatrics department of the Medical Center for what was believed to be arthritis not responsive to usual treatment. He was newly diagnosed as having leukemia and was referred to the Oncology Clinic. At the same time the initial work-up was done, a diagnosis of neurofibromatosis* also was made in the father and Roberto. This diagnosis has not been shared as yet with the family. The social worker is concerned and wondering if the family needs genetic counseling at this time.

The problem is further complicated by the social history of the family and the fact that the mother is currently two months pregnant. The family is Catholic, and they speak only Spanish. The social worker is fluent in Spanish, but the doctors are not. Mr. G. wants the current pregnancy aborted, Mrs. G. does not. The parents had been separated for several years and only recently reconciled. Mr. G. reportedly deserted the marriage, leaving Mrs. G. to care for their sons Tony and Roberto and their daughter Maria. Mrs. G. worked as a waitress to support the family until the father's recent return. During Mr. G.'s absence, Tony was ill with leukemia and died two years ago, at 14. Maria is now age 11. The G.'s currently are having considerable marital difficulty, and Mrs. G. talks about "throwing him out."

The social worker reports that the doctor mentioned to her, "in passing," that the family should have genetic counseling. Her questions relate to when and how this should occur, if at all.

This case demonstrates the many practice issues that may complicate making a referral to genetic counseling. Issues of whether or not to refer, the timing of such referral, and goals of referral surface in the context of the multiproblem, family situation. The most immediate concern of the family is most likely the making of the diagnosis of leukemia in a second child in the family. The social worker's first task needs to be focused on helping the family members deal with this diagnostic crisis. Nevertheless, the mother's pregnancy introduces another source of possible urgency in relation to genetic counseling. On the other hand, a referral for genetic counseling at this time would likely be a source of added stress at an already strained period. Indeed, one questions how receptive Mrs. G. could be to the genetic counseling if so much of her energies are focused on Roberto's diagnosis of leukemia.

In order to proceed the social worker needs much more information from the physician who asked for the referral to be made. Why now? What are his reasons for the referral? How really urgent is it that the family learn about the neurofibromatosis? It seems more likely that the genetic question of most urgency to the family concerns the possible genetic factors at work in causing leukemia in a second son. Can the physician shed light on this question and discuss this with the family? In addition, the social worker needs to assess the family's vulnerability to further stress, the possible impact of this additional diagnosis on the G. family in their current situation, and in particular their ability to understand and make use of genetic counseling if a referral were to be made at this point. The ability to make such assessments rests, however, on the social worker having a clear understanding of the genetic and health implications of neurofibromatosis.

In this case it was important for the worker to know that the genetic problem, neurofibromatosis, is an autosomal dominant disorder, thereby confirming that the father has transmitted the disease to Roberto. In view of the strained marital situation, the social worker may need to assess how this information will be used by the wife. In addition, however, it is important to evaluate the likelihood of the couple drawing their own conclusions about the inheritance of the disease if the fact that father and son have the disease is shared with them. The extreme variability in the severity of neurofibromatosis lends another layer of ambiguity to the situation. If the father and Roberto have experienced any serious complications, the mother is more likely to be quite frightened about the risk to her unborn fetus. On the other hand, if the father and son have not experienced any major problems, it may be very difficult for the family to contemplate the serious medical problems that can accompany neurofibromatosis. In the latter case, the question arises as to how much emphasis to place on discussing the most negative possibilities.

The mother's pregnancy speaks to some urgency as the recurrence risk for neurofibromatosis is 50% for each pregnancy. It would also be important for the social worker to assess carefully the basis for the mother's opposition to abortion. The genetic information may reinforce the conflict that exists between the parents over the current pregnancy. Appropriate sharing of such assessments with the genetic counselors might emerge as a significant factor in the referral process. An ethical issue arises out of the question of to whom this genetic information (the diagnosis) belongs? How this question is answered will determine what the family is told. The decision on referral for genetic counseling similarly is dependent on the response to the frequently debated question of whether individuals and their families should be informed about the implications of all available medical information.

PRACTICE ISSUES IN FIELDS OTHER THAN HEALTH CARE

Dilemmas generated by the new genetic knowledge and technology will be increasingly significant to clinical social work practice in fields other than the health arena. Questions related to reproduction in the face of known or suspected genetic risks are likely to be focal points for serious discussion in premarital and marital counseling. The impact of genetic disease on individual and family functioning presents new challenges in the social treatment of clients in family service agencies. With the increasing knowledge and awareness about genetic factors in schizophrenia, affective disorders, and alcoholism (Tsuang & VanderMey, 1980), the mental health field will need to address the issue of providing psychiatric genetic counseling to affected individuals and their families. Much work will be needed to identify the specific issues in these and other fields of practice where genetic implications and concerns have an impact on many aspects of psychosocial functioning.

An example of this kind of work is seen in the exploratory examination of the effects of the new clinical genetics on the field of adoptions. Black (1983) has identified four areas of potential impact of genetic issues on adoption policies and practices: (1) the adoptive placement of children who are the product of incestuous matings; (2) situations involving the discovery of a genetic problem that has major medical implications in an adoptee or in one of the biological parents; (3) potential implications of genetic heritage in placing adoptees whose family histories include psychiatric illness, alcoholism, or psychopathic behavior; and (4) moving to another level, the importance of one's biological and genetic heritage for a personal sense of identity. The adoption worker is faced with many conflicts related to these areas. What should be done when a child is known to be a product of an incestuous union, or the even more ambiguous situation in which incest is strongly suspected but cannot be proven? Genetic risks that the offspring will develop health problems may run high. Truly informed decision making on the part of adoptive parents is one absolute in such situations. The social worker should see that complete information on the genetic risks is made available to all parties involved. Potential adoptive parents need to be engaged in thorough and open discussion of the genetic issues as a prelude to any adoption decision.

In dealing with the situations that arise after an adoption is completed, there are two closely related issues: confidentiality and the nature of the data to be obtained on the biological families. These issues involve legal considerations of informed consent and just cause for opening sealed records. Direct service workers are called on to conduct preplacement investigations and contact relatives if critical information arises at a later date. To execute professionally such tasks requires basic knowledge of: (1) the basic principles of human genetics and modes of inheritance; (2) the nature of genetic counseling services and referral procedures to the closest genetic clinic; and (3) the major psychosocial tasks likely to be faced by individuals or families confronting genetic diagnoses. Throughout all such work, moreover, social workers must give careful attention and study to both sides of the "nature-nurture" debate. For there are no true "either/or" answers, but rather a complex interweaving of innate vulnerabilities and potentials, that, in interaction with equally powerful environmental forces, influence the course of an individual's development. Especially in the case of psychiatric illnesses, practical questions of adoption workers still remain unanswered: (1) To whom should information on psychiatric problems in a family history be given—to the adopting parents only or to the adoptee directly? (2) At what age should the adoptee be told? (3) Is it the worker's responsibility to point out the possibility of an increased risk for a psychiatric disorder in a child's family history if the prospective parents do not express any concerns about it?

The growing knowledge available about genetic disorders and genetic counseling services suggests that the wide psychosocial ramifications of human genetics are likely to emerge with increasing frequency in other fields of social work practice. Two important tasks for social work will be: (1) to clearly articulate the nature of these new challenges for clients and (2) to develop practice approaches for assisting individuals and families in their coping efforts.

NOTES

1. Although the genetic pedigree is perhaps unique to genetic services, the similar process frequently employed by social workers of drawing a family tree or "genogram" also has been found to be a helpful therapeutic tool (see discussion in Chapter 3).

2. The discussion in the next two sections is drawn largely from Black (1981).

3. Vespa (1977) gives recognition to the fact that alternative beliefs about health, the causes of disease, and healing are found in both rural and urban areas and among such ethnic groups as American blacks, Pennsylvania Dutch, Appalachian whites, Sicilian Americans, and gypsies.

4. Although both examples provided in the text are taken from practice experiences with Mexican-American couples, the general issues discussed in this section apply across the many different cultural traditions and beliefs about health and disease.

6

Genetic Screening: Historical Development and Policy Issues

The object of screening for disease is to discover those among the apparently well who are in fact suffering from disease. They can then be placed under treatment and, if the disease is communicable, steps can be taken to prevent them from being a danger to their neighbours. In theory, therefore, screening is an admirable method of combating disease, since it should help detect it in its early stages and enable it to be treated adequately before it obtains a firm hold on the community. In practice, there are snags. (Wilson & Jungner, 1968)

In this chapter we consider those genetic services known as genetic screening. Up to this point, the main focus has been on the impact of genetic diagnoses, the genetic counseling process, and the practice concerns involved in helping individuals and families cope with genetic disorders and their implications. Genetic screening, in contrast, arises from a public health perspective that emphasizes prevention of genetic disease through the active search for genetically affected or at-risk individuals or populations. Genetic screening efforts have become a significant resource for detecting genetic disease in the population and for early identification of individuals and families who could benefit from genetic counseling services.

The opening quotation of this chapter describes general medical screening with its historical focus on mass screening for such communicable diseases as malaria, syphilis, and tuberculosis. But if, as Wilson and Jungner (1968) suggest, medical screening has had its "snags," genetic screening has had even more. Although genetic disease is "in a very special sense, communicable" across generations (Powledge, 1974, p. 27), much of current screening to prevent genetic disease and its spread does not lead to clear cures, treatments, or the genetic equivalent of vaccinations. Although dramatic exceptions do exist, as in treatment for phenylketonuria (PKU),* described below, and experimental treatment procedures such as fetal surgery (Henig, 1982), genetic screening remains a public health effort that frequently may raise more questions for its recipients than it answers.

More and more people are participating in various types of genetic screening efforts. Newborn screening, carrier detection programs, and prenatal diagnostic procedures are forms of genetic screening that now touch a large proportion of the population; the increasing interest of industry in genetic screening of its workers (Severo, 1980, 1982) suggests we are only beginning to see the uses of these technologies. As a result of these tests, many individuals are being confronted with the often unexpected need to face genetic issues in their personal lives. Clinical social work services can be utilized to advantage to assist individuals in coping with the implications of genetic screening programs. Moreover, as we hope to demonstrate in this chapter, it is equally important for social workers to begin to assume active roles in the planning, delivery, and evaluation of these programs. As the history of genetic screening demonstrates, failure to consider the potentially significant psychological, social, and legal ramifications of genetic screening not only mars the effectiveness of such public health efforts but also can result in troublesome and painful outcomes for participants.

NEWBORN SCREENING: THE PKU STORY

Genetic screening formally began only about 20 years ago with the institution of large-scale testing of newborns for phenylketonuria (PKU). PKU is an autosomal recessive disorder caused by a defect in an enzyme (phenylalanine hydroxylase), which normally metabolizes the amino acid phenylalanine. The discovery of PKU in 1934 by Folling marked the first demonstration of a genetic defect as a cause of mental retardation (Thompson & Thompson, 1980). The enzyme blockage results in increased levels of phenylalanine in the body and usually leads to severe and irreversible intellectual deterioration. A diet low in phenylalanine begun shortly after birth usually can prevent this decline and allow the development of normal intellectual functioning in the child. PKU is reported to have an incidence of about 1 in 10,000 births in North America, resulting in a carrier incidence of about one in 50, although a higher frequency is found among populations of northern European descent (Thompson & Thompson, 1980). (See Schild, 1979, for a complete discussion of the psychosocial impact of PKU in families.)

Because children with PKU appear normal at birth and become retarded only when they ingest excess phenylalanine, PKU rapidly became a prototype for mass screening of newborn populations for such inborn errors of metabolism. Following the introduction of a simple and inexpensive screening test in 1961, the era of high quality, low cost mass genetic screening began (Reilly, 1978). Despite some professional disagreement about the diagnosis and treatment of PKU, the new test was seized upon by many concerned citizens, scientists, and politicians who campaigned successfully to institute newborn screening for PKU (Bessman & Swazey, 1971). In 1963 Massachusetts became the first state to *require* that the PKU test be performed on all newborns. Within 5 years, 42 other states enacted similar laws, while the other states developed voluntary programs (Powledge, 1974).

Reilly (1977) has forcefully described the rapid, unreflective process by which *mandatory* PKU screening laws were passed. Technical and medical difficulties in the procedures frequently were overlooked. For example, legislation ignored the fact that because the introduction of the special diet can be dangerous for a normal infant, and a high rate of false positive results is inevitable in any screening test, careful follow-up studies and repeat testing must be built into all programs. Moreover, few of the original laws required that parents be informed about the tests, that genetic counseling be offered to parents of affected babies, that screening records be kept confidential, or that children with PKU be guaranteed competent care.

These oversights become more understandable when one realizes the well-intentioned enthusiasm with which lawmakers jumped at this new opportunity actually to find and to treat a disease that would otherwise cause severe mental retardation. The genetic nature of the disorder was not even known by many (Swazey, 1971). As a treatable disorder, PKU seemingly fell into the traditional pattern of public health efforts to screen for treatable medical problems. While many of the oversights would have applied to any public health screening program, failure to consider the genetic implications of PKU proved particularly troublesome. An opportunity to address the difficult issues involved in establishing a model for future genetic screening programs was missed, but the underlying problems could not be avoided for long. As the next wave of legislation for sickle cell disease was soon to prove, failure to provide careful legislative review of genetic screening programs could lead to serious and harmful results.

SCREENING FOR "CARRIERS": THE INTRODUCTION OF A NEW BIOLOGICAL AND SOCIAL STATUS

The late 1960s . . . witnessed a movement toward a completely different kind of screening, aimed not at the diseased homozygote but at the carrier heterozygote; not just at the eradication of disease but the eradication of babies with the disease. Kass (1973) has asked, "In the case of what other disease does preventive medicine consist in the elimination of the patient-at-risk?" . . . It can hardly be over-stressed (because it has been so frequently ignored) that this movement represented a brand new step in screening, one that might legitimately be called the ultimate in preventive medicine. (Powledge, 1974, pp. 33–34)

The major focus of heterozygote screening in this country during the early 1970s was largely on two diseases: sickle cell disease, also referred to as sickle cell anemia, and Tay-Sachs disease. The differences and similarities in the development of these programs illustrate important lessons for social workers.

Sickle Cell Disease

Sickle cell disease is a severe blood disorder characterized by a tendency of the red blood cells to become grossly abnormal in shape, i.e., "sickled cells," under conditions of low oxygen. Affected individuals may suffer from anemia, jaundice, and "sickle cell crises" that occur when the sickled cells clog the vessels and cause painful and destructive blockages of blood flow to various parts of the body. Sickle cell disease, like PKU, is inherited as an autosomal recessive disorder. Parents of affected children are heterozygotes, i.e., carriers of one altered gene. They are said to have *sickle cell trait* and are usually totally healthy. About 8% of American blacks have the sickle cell trait, but it is also not uncommon in many nonblack populations, including southern Italians and Sicilians, northern Greeks, and central and south Indians. Although sickle cell disease usually is a severe, debilitating, and often fatal disease in early childhood, treatment is improving, and patients are living longer and more comfortable lives (Thompson & Thompson, 1980).

Throughout the early years of sickle cell screening, no type of prenatal diagnosis was available for the disease. Thus knowledge of carrier status in couples could be used only in deciding for or against taking the 25% risk of having an affected child in each pregnancy. As described in Chapter 3, a new biochemical method recently has become available for prenatal diagnosis, but in view of the uncertain and possibly improved prognosis for those with the disease, the place of prenatal diagnosis for sickle cell disease remains a matter of uncertain benefit to many families.

Although long known by medical scientists, sickle cell disease rose to political prominence in 1970 and thereby marked the beginning of a second round of genetic screening laws. That year a major article (Scott, 1970) and editorial, appearing simultaneously in the *Journal of the American Medical Association*, made strong pleas for provision of sickle cell screening and counseling programs for the black population. Shortly afterwards, in 1971, President Nixon urged more funding for sickle cell research, and once again, Massachusetts led the way in becoming the first of 13 states to write *mandatory* sickle cell screening laws during 1971 and 1972.

Like the PKU laws, the sickle cell statutes were enacted rapidly and with little reflection. However, unlike the PKU testing experience, the benefits of sickle cell screening did not win out over the poorly drafted legislation (Reilly, 1978). Immediately apparent were such glaring errors as confusing carrier status with the disease state itself and failing to mandate the use of the most sensitive testing methods available. Further examination of these laws revealed even more basic and fundamental shortcomings which, if left unchanged, would have served as dangerous precedents for future genetic screening legislation. These flaws, which repeated some of the errors seen in the earlier PKU legislation, included (Reilly, 1977):

1. Mandatory screening. This was a particularly distressing policy in view of the targeting of the black population for this test and the likely targeting of other racial groups in future carrier detection programs.
2. Confusing sickle cell disease with communicable diseases such as syphilis. In many cases the sickle cell programs were simply added to already existing public health laws without thought to the increased potential for social stigmatization involved in linking sickle cell with communicable diseases.
3. Lack of provision for adequate follow-up counseling.
4. Failure to guard against the potentials for stigmatization and discrimination by instituting public education programs to counteract such misunderstanding.
5. Lack of provision for protection of confidentiality of the genetic screening data.

Criticism mounted even as these laws were being passed in the individual states, for it quickly became clear that the objective of sickle cell screening laws was radically different from that of earlier PKU or other medical screening laws. Suddenly the new focus was on alerting *healthy* individuals about the possible risks for childbearing. No treatment of disease was being offered, and the major participants were not sick. The negative impact of these laws has been chronicled in detail (Reilly, 1977). In some states, children were barred from school until they had been tested, thereby adding to the confusion of sickle cell disease with communicable diseases. Some adults who were found to be carriers experienced disruptions in marriages, higher insurance costs, and discrimination in hiring. Not surprisingly perhaps, fears of genocide also were kindled in the black population.

The National Sickle Cell Anemia Control Act, enacted in 1972 and later expanded in 1976 as the National Genetic Disease Act, was one attempt to correct some of these errors. Its guidelines for screening programs include voluntary participation, strict confidentiality of test results, community representation in the provision of genetic services, and guarantee of genetic counseling to persons found to have sickle cell disease. Unfortunately these guidelines came only after considerable damage had been done as a result of this first unsuccessful and negative episode in our legislative and social response to genetic disease. A more detailed discussion of guidelines for genetic screening programs follows later in this chapter.

Tay-Sachs Screening: A Model for Community Participation

The development of screening programs for Tay-Sachs disease stands in sharp contrast to the mishandling of sickle cell screening. Tay-Sachs disease, another autosomal recessive disorder, involves a marked deficiency of the enzyme hexosaminidase A. This enzyme normally degrades certain fatty substances in cells. In its absence, this fatty substance accumulates, especially in brain tissue. The affected infant appears normal until about 6 months of age but then begins a progressive mental and physical decline that leads to death in early childhood. Parents, who are heterozygote carriers, are totally healthy but can be identified with a screening test. Unlike PKU, no treatment is available for an affected child, but prenatal testing is possible for identifying the affected fetus and termination of pregnancy if so desired.

Although very rare in the general population (1/360,000), Tay-Sachs is much more frequent among Ashkenazi Jews where the frequency is 100 times higher: 1 in 3,600 affected with one in 30 as carriers. Because of these features—high frequency in a clearly delineated population group, feasibility of mass screening of carriers, and the possibility of prenatal diagnosis—Tay-Sachs has become the prototype for carrier screening to prevent devastating inborn errors of metabolism (Thompson & Thompson, 1980).

In comparing the Tay-Sachs and sickle cell experiences, striking differences emerge in the planning and organization of the two testing programs (Powledge, 1974). While not totally free of criticism (Goodman & Goodman, 1982; Holtzman, 1977), the Tay-Sachs programs from the outset have been voluntary and based on enlisting the support and enthusiasm of various Jewish organizations. The screening programs have generally conveyed an impression of being carefully planned and organized, with a great deal of emphasis on community education and involvement (Kaback, 1977; Massarik & Kaback, 1981; Powledge, 1974).

Psychosocial Implications of Carrier Screening

Relatively few data are available about the social and psychological impact of genetic screening for carriers (Kenen & Schmidt, 1978; Scotch & Sorenson, 1977). The early mishandling of sickle cell screening provided a painful lesson in the importance of considering the potential negative psychosocial and economic consequences of carrier detection programs. One prospective study that has been completed on this subject involved a small farming village of Orchemenos in Greece (Stamatoyannopoulos, 1974) where 23% of the population are sickle-cell carriers and 1% of babies are born with the disease. A follow-up study conducted 7 years after screening the population and counseling the villagers revealed that people identified as carriers held a socially stigmatized status. Individuals frequently attempted to keep their carrier status a secret, and, in fact, the number of carrier-carrier matings was the same as would have been expected by random marriage. Caution, of course, must be exercised in applying the results from a small, closely knit, rural community to a largely urbanized and industralized society. A stigmatized status may not develop as easily in the more anonymous context of large metropolitan areas. Nevertheless, the possibility of such repercussions must be considered in the planning of any genetic screening effort.

Tay-Sachs screening programs, in contrast, seem to have had generally quite positive outcomes (Kaback, 1977; Massarik & Kaback, 1981). The majority of participants have been enthusiastic about the screening. Preliminary data indicate that little stigmatization has resulted and that there have been no adverse changes in interpersonal relationships or reproductive planning (Childs, Gordis, Kaback, & Kazazian, 1976). Similar positive results also have been reported in a study of relatives who were sought out and counseled after the discovery that a relative had hemophilia or muscular dystrophy (Lubs & delaCruz, 1977).

Uncertain and sometimes contradictory data have emerged about the psychosocial impact of carrier screening programs, and research has not yet determined the specific factors that make one screening program a helpful service while another becomes a source of stigma and anguish. It thus seems reasonable to accept the observation made by Kenen and Schmidt (1978) that with this new technology we may have introduced:

a new biological and social label—"carrier"—with yet unknown psychological and social consequences. We do not have any direct, cultural experience with a stigmatized carrier status or any cultural traditions to guide us. The newly identified carriers of mutant alleles are, in a sense, both biological and social pioneers. (pp. 1117–1118)

PRENATAL DIAGNOSIS

Prenatal diagnosis stands as the third type of testing that can be considered a form of genetic screening. Not only is it inextricably intertwined with carrier detection programs such as for sickle cell and Tay-Sachs disease, but in recent years has become available as a genetic screening service for women 35 years and older who are at risk for disorders of chromosome nondisjunction, such as Down syndrome. Prenatal diagnosis differs greatly from carrier detection programs, however, in that it screens only for an already affected fetus. Termination of the pregnancy thus becomes the major means of "prevention" available, although the experimental use of fetal surgery in selected disorders holds promise for the expansion of possibilities for medical intervention.

The use of prenatal diagnosis, primarily by amniocentesis, to detect abnormalities has increased rapidly in the last decade. New York State demonstrates this trend particularly well. Between 1977 and 1978, the number of diagnoses increased by 47%, and between 1978 and 1979 there was another 49% increase (Hook, Schreinemachers, & Cross, 1981). These increases translate into a statewide utilization rate of 28.7% in 1979 for pregnant women 35 or older and a rate of 33% for New York City.

Increased availability and the documented safety of the procedure (NICHD Study Group, 1976) undoubtedly have contributed to the increased use of prenatal diagnosis. Public awareness of the procedure also seems to be increasing. In a survey of 1,616 women aged 30 to 45 in upstate New York, 85% knew of the existence of a prenatal test for birth defects, although they did lack detailed knowledge about the procedure or for whom its use was most appropriate (Sell, Roghmann, & Doherty, 1978).

Despite these dramatic increases in utilization, it appears that less than 50% of pregnant women who could use prenatal testing are receiving it. The average utilization rate nationally for women 35 years and older was 18% in 1979–80, with the rate varying from 5–49% across different programs (Sepe, Oakley, & Manley, 1981). Moreover, urban women and white women seem to use prenatal testing more frequently than do black and rural residents (Adams, Finley, Hansen, Jahiel, Oakley, Sanger, Wells, & Wertelecki, 1981). Extensive data are lacking on the factors contributing to these differentials in utilization rates, but at least one study has demonstrated that acceptance of amniocentesis is not limited to white, middle-class patients. This investigation, which was conducted in Atlanta, Georgia, found that 61% of low-income, black patients who were offered the procedure accepted it (Marion, Kassam, Farnhoff, Brantley, Carroll, Zacharias, Klein, Priest, & Elsas, 1980).

In view of the increasing use of prenatal testing, it is important to consider its psychosocial consequences and risks. As discussed in Chapter 4, research on the impact of amniocentesis indicates that there is a certain degree of anxiety connected with the procedure, although for most individuals, the testing experience does not seem to represent a major crisis. More significant problems have emerged for the small minority who receive news of a serious defect in the fetus. The experiences of such families provide a painful reminder that despite hopes for prenatal treatment, the primary rationale for prenatal diagnosis as a form of genetic screening is termination of a pregnancy in which a defect is detected, and, in fact, the majority of couples with positive results do elect abortion.

We thus find ourselves a long distance from the early enthusiasm of the 1960s and its rush to institute PKU screening: genetic screening that resulted in a "cure" that prevented at least one type of mental retardation. As we have seen, that initial euphoria soon evaporated as the full implications of carrier testing emerged. Although it provides extremely valuable and much wanted information, the only prevention offered by carrier screening is that provided by prevention or selected termination of pregnancies to carrier couples. Prenatal diagnosis stands now as the latest strategy in society's efforts to "prevent" genetic disease. Again, although it provides relief from anxiety for most at-risk couples and spares others from the burdens of caring for an affected child, prenatal diagnosis offers no easy answers or cures.

GUIDELINES FOR GENETIC SCREENING PROGRAMS

In the mid-1970s the Division of Medical Sciences of the National Research Council, National Academy of Sciences, commissioned a Committee for the Study of Inborn Errors of Metabolism. The rapid rise in genetic screening programs and the errors that were made in the early efforts suggested the "need for a review of current screening practices . . . [that would] give some procedural guidance, in order to minimize the shortcomings and maximize the effectiveness of future genetic screening programs" (Committee, 1975, p. iii). In addition to a lengthy and comprehensive report on a range of issues in genetic screening, the Committee made a series of very specific recommendations for the conduct of such programs.[1]

The Committee's recommendations covered not only general considerations but also specific organizational, educational, legal, and research concerns. Overall, the Committee judged that genetic screening was an

SOCIAL WORK AND GENETICS

120

appropriate form of medical care but only when stringent requirements were met; these included: evidence of substantial benefits; provision of appropriate public education, counseling, and follow-up; and adequate means to evaluate the effectiveness and success of each step in the screening process. Organizational considerations emphasized the essential nature of public representation in the design and operation of these programs, with fully open disclosure of the aims of the screening. Standardization of techniques and regionalization were suggested as important to insure evenness in quality and equal access to testing for residents in states with low population densities. The Committee viewed education of the public about genetic disorders as of primary importance in fostering appropriate conceptions of susceptibility to and seriousness of genetic disease and carrier status. Legal guidelines emphasized the necessity of voluntary participation and protection of confidentiality in the handling of all records. Research in genetic screening should follow the most rigorous standards and should include investigation of the social and ethical ramifications of screening in the lives of the persons tested. Table 11 provides detailed excerpts taken directly from the Committee's recommendations.

TABLE 11
Recommendations for Genetic Screening Programs

General

— *Genetic screening, when carried out under controlled conditions, is an appropriate form of medical care, when the following criteria are met:*

   a. There is evidence of substantial public benefit and acceptance, including acceptance by medical practitioners.

   b. Its feasiblility has been investigated, and it has been found that benefits outweigh costs; appropriate public education can be carried out; test methods are satisfactory; laboratory facilities are available; and resources exist to deal with counseling, follow-up, and other consequences of testing.

   c. An investigative pretest of the program has shown that costs are acceptable; education is effective; informed consent is feasible; aims of the program with regard to the size of the sample to be screened, the age of the screenees, and the setting in which the testing is to be done have been defined; laboratory facilities have been shown to fulfill requirements for quality control; techniques for communicating results are workable; qualified and effective counselors are available in sufficient number; and adequate provision for effective services have been made.

   d. The means are available to evaluate the effectiveness and success of each step in the process.

Organizational

— *Responsibility for the organization and control of genetic screening programs should be lodged in some agency representative of both the public and the health professions.* This is necessary because of the public nature of genetic screening and its use of public

TABLE 11 (continued)

facilities. It is also essential because such screening carries some potential for invasion of privacy, "labeling," breach of confidentiality, and psychological abuse. The agency might take its authority from local or state government or from regional representation of a federal program.

— *Public representation is necessary both in determining that a new screening program is clearly in the public interest and also in the design and operation of any such program . . .*

— *The aims of genetic screening should be clearly formulated and spelled out by the initiators of any screening program and should be publicly articulated with precision and candor.* Thus there will be no possibility of a mistaken impression that the program is intended to be an instrument of discrimination or is devoted to any "eugenic" cause.

— *Some degree of standardization of screening projects is desirable.* Demographic diversity, inequality of financial and educational resources of the various states, and the individuality of initiators of screening projects all lead to variation in the design, quality, and cost of screening programs. Standardization might be achieved by some national agency that could act as a clearinghouse for ideas and techniques, set standards, and exert quality control.

— *Regional programs with laboratories and other facilities based on population numbers rather than political subdivisions should be developed to make screening services of high quality available equally to all.* Such programs would avoid the low priority currently given to genetic screening in states of low population density and low budget and would prevent the hardship otherwise suffered by the relatively few persons in such states to whom screening would be beneficial.

— *In the future, genetic screening should be regarded as one among several preventive health measures and its development should take place in the context of the evolution of health care in general.* New projects should be dictated by general principles governing genetic screening rather than by pressures originating in the special qualities of particular diseases.

Educational

— *It is essential to begin the study of human biology, including genetics and probability, in primary school, continuing with a more health-related curriculum in secondary school because:*

 a. In the absence of sufficient public knowledge of human biology and genetics, the difficulties of arousing concern over genetic diseases cannot be overcome, since even longstanding attempts to educate the public regarding traditional preventive health measures have had variable success.

 b. In the short run, the educational aspects of genetic screening must consist of special campaigns devoted to each program. Sufficient knowledge of genetics, probability, and medicine leading to appropriate perceptions of susceptibility to and seriousness of genetic disease and carrier status cannot be acquired as a consequence of incidental, accidental, or haphazard learning.

— *Screening authorities could improve the effectiveness of public education by studying and employing methods devised and tested by professional students of health behavior and health education.* The use of mass communication media and other techniques to change attitudes and behavior has not been particularly successful, partly because of failure to follow the appropriate precepts . . .

— *Schools of medicine, public health and hygiene, and allied health sciences, as well as universities, should receive support for programs to set standards and train persons to*

SOCIAL WORK AND GENETICS

TABLE 11 (continued)

inform and counsel participants in screening programs. Such counselors are already in short supply.

Legal

— *Participation in a genetic screening program should not be made mandatory by law, but should be left to the discretion of the person tested or, if a minor, of the parents or legal guardian.*
— *Identifying information obtained through genetic screening should not be made available to anyone other than the screenee except with the permission of the screenee or, in the case of a minor, with the permission of the parents or legal guardian.*
— *Screening authorities should consult regularly with lawyers and other persons knowledgeable in ethics to avoid social consequences of screening that may be damaging.* These take the form of invasion of privacy, breach of confidentiality, and other transgressions of civil rights, as well as psychological damage resulting from being "labeled" or from misunderstandings about the significance of diseases and carrier states. The usefulness of or need for legislation to protect the participants in screening programs from such dangers should be reviewed from time to time . . .

Research

— *Research in genetic screening should be governed by the rigorous standards employed in laboratory investigation.* Special efforts should be made to evaluate all aspects, even of routine procedures, and the social and ethical ramifications of screening in the lives of the persons tested should be investigated. So far, experience in genetic screening is insufficient to foresee and to forestall all possible untoward side effects. Accordingly, it should be approached in an experimental mood. At present, it is impressions that prevail, rather than data collected and analyzed according to scientific rules . . .

(Excerpts taken from the Recommendations, Committee for the Study of Inborn Errors of Metabolism, 1975, pp. 1–5)

FUTURE PROSPECTS:
SCREENING FOR GENETIC VULNERABILITY—
A CHANGING CONCEPT OF DISEASE

Genetic screening in the United States has had a brief but turbulent history. Major errors were committed in the rush to institute PKU and sickle-cell screening programs. Much has been learned from those early mistakes, however, and the more detailed scrutiny now being given to these issues offers some hope that future developments in genetic screening will result in more thoughtfully constructed and implemented programs and policies.

The importance of realizing this hope becomes especially clear if we consider briefly what the present and near future may hold for developments in genetic screening. Increasingly sophisticated and knowledgeable policy will be needed, for we are on the verge of no less than the beginning of a basic change in our definition of illness (Powledge, 1974). In this new definition, the traditional distinctions between genetic and non-genetic disorders are becoming blurred. Genetic factors in such common disorders as heart disease, high blood pressure, and diabetes have been revealed, and medicine is moving rapidly to a view of differential "genetic susceptibility" as a basic characteristic of all people in relation to their environments. In a sense then, screening for elevated cholesterol or high blood pressure can be called genetic screening. As Powledge (1974) has described it, this new perspective views all disease as potential and dependent for its development on a push from its surroundings.

> Should diseases be likened to ivy growing on the oak tree or are they part of the oak tree itself? Should diseases be regarded as human analogues of defects in an internal-combustion engine or a Swiss watch, or should they be regarded as psychobiological expressions of man evolving within the constraints and potentials contributed from his aliquot of society's gene pool? Are diseases "things" that "happen" to people, or are they manifestations of constructive or destructive relations of individuals in their social and physical environment? (White, 1973, p. 25)

The implications of this new perspective hold both highly positive as well as problematic implications. A most immediate problem, one that is already at hand, stems from the seemingly benign goal of altering the environment of the genetically susceptible to prevent or to ameliorate physical dysfunction. Such attention to the person in interaction with the environment is a familiar domain for social workers. But prior experiences have also educated us to the twin dangers of "blaming the victim" and of choosing the easy way out of a difficult environment, of defining the "problem" as belonging to the individual rather than attempting the more difficult, but often ultimately more beneficial, task of modifying the environment to suit the needs of the individual better.

One specific test of this new genetic perspective has arisen over the issue of genetic screening in industrial settings (Powledge, 1976; Severo, 1980, 1982). A number of companies have developed genetic screening programs based on uncertain scientific evidence of increased risk and prior to establishing clear policies for protection of confidentiality in employee records or even for determining whether and how test results are to be used (Severo, 1980). That such negligence should continue to occur after this society's experience with the sickle-cell screening programs raises significant questions about the efficacy of safeguards for future screening efforts. Even putting aside, however, the procedural mishandling of these specific industrial programs, one is still left with the dilemma of how to respond to our increasing ability to screen the population for genetically based differences in vulnerability to certain environments.

Once again, concepts familiar to social workers such as "high risk screening" and "reasonable accommodation" for the disabled would seem to apply. The difficult question, put bluntly by Powledge (1976), seems to be: "should workers be selected for their genetic 'immunity' to hazards or should the work environment be made safe for all workers by eliminating hazards" (p. 486). Is it reasonable to expect companies to "accommodate" to even the most "genetically vulnerable," or are there "reasonable" limits to what society can afford to ask them to do?

In spite of such already present dangers inherent in a broadened view of genetic vulnerability, the potentially positive impact of this new perspective should not be underestimated. Our increasing knowledge about genetic variables in many of our common and not so common illnesses holds much promise for ultimately eliminating the many special concerns about genetic screening that we have been addressing. As long as genetic disorders are labeled as somehow stranger and rarer than other medical problems, stigma, fear, and controversy are likely to remain attached to genetic screening and genetic diagnoses in general. The potential exists now for a significant shift toward a perspective that views genetic disorders as no more "interesting" or stigmatizing than other health problems. As newborn and prenatal screening programs expand to include a wide variety of genetic as well as nongenetic disorders and as attention to inherited predispositions to a variety of ailments becomes a more routine part of primary medical care, it is hoped that genetic screening will become less and less a target of special concern.

ROLES FOR SOCIAL WORK

Review of the history and future prospects of genetic screening in the United States provides another example of the interweaving of public and private issues that social workers have long recognized as a significant focus of the work of the profession (Schwartz, 1969). These concerns are dramatized perhaps most effectively through a case example. Although the following situation specifically addresses the issues of only one particular disorder, it nevertheless highlights the wide range of practice implications that genetic screening holds for social work.

Mr. and Mrs. R. came into the office to discuss their son, Paul, who is diagnosed as having G6PD deficiency.* Paul, who was away in the U.S. military at the time of the first appointment, had first learned of his G6PD deficiency after being screened during basic training. Mr. and Mrs. R. were interested in knowing more about G6PD, as it had never been thoroughly explained to them or their son. It was also discovered, after further testing initiated by the R.'s, that Paul's younger sister also has the deficiency.

One concern that the R.'s expressed, after learning more about the disorder, was the fact that their son was assigned to a unit that had the potential for duty in the Mediterranean, a malarial-belt region. This would necessitate that Paul be treated with antimalarial drugs that could potentially bring on hemolytic problems secondary to his G6PD deficiency. They also worried about the fact that the military had not explained anything about the condition to their son after it was identified in the screening.

Mr. and Mrs. R., with permission from their son, contracted with the social worker to act as their son's patient advocate. Paul, who wished to remain in the military, agreed that two requests be made of the military: (1) that Paul be given a geographic restriction that would ensure that he not be sent to countries in which he would require antimalarial drugs, and (2) that Paul's medical record be amended to include the information that the social worker provided for Paul on G6PD deficiency. This information included a list of malarial-belt regions as well as a list of drugs that would be contraindicated for people with G6PD deficiency. Such information was not in Paul's medical record at that time.

The attempt to rectify these two concerns was a lengthy and very distressing process for Paul, his family, and his social worker. Initially, the medic for the unit was contacted by the social worker. He directed the matter to the medical officer, but after this point there seemed to be no further movement in having the situation addressed. Between the months of January and June, the R. family enlisted the assistance of the American Red Cross Services to Armed Forces Families, their local congressman's office, the state attorney general's office, and the state senator's office. The military's seeming lack of interest in the welfare of this enlistee made it necessary to involve these people. There was no response to the correspondence that was directed to the military by Paul and his family, and their request to meet with Paul's commanding officer was denied. Paul came under increasing pressure from his superiors for "stirring up trouble." He also became increasingly worried about the status of his health should his unit be sent to the Mediterranean as scheduled in one year. He did not want to be forced into the position of violating military orders by refusing to go but felt he would have to do this if he was not able to obtain the geographic restriction. The stress that Paul was under was beginning to affect his military performance.

Finally, after months elapsed without achieving anything, the R. family decided to contact a friend at a local TV news station who arranged to tell their story on the local news. It was this broadcast that finally precipitated pressure being put on the military by the local congressman to address this serviceman's concerns. With the assistance of a military hematologist and the patient affairs officer, Paul was given a medical discharge in October. After discharge, Paul and his family obtained a lawyer to address the following issues:

1. Was it necessary for Paul to be discharged instead of being given a geographic restriction as was requested? Is he possibly being denied money that he might be entitled to?
2. Due to the fact that Paul's was a preexisting condition, is it legal to deny him military benefits that he might otherwise be entitled to?

The genetic service identified the following concerns about the military's screening procedures for G6PD deficiency:

1. Screening seems to have been done with no therapeutic recommendations.
2. Screening was done with no educational process.
3. The goals of screening were unclear.
4. Screening apparently was done without truly informed consent.

This genetic screening clearly failed to follow any of the suggested guidelines (Committee, 1975). The consequences for the young man of this failure underscore the imperatives that developers of guidelines clearly have recognized; genetic screening programs must be developed with careful attention to their psychological, social, and legal implications.

In the above vignette, the social worker's role is identified clearly as that of advocate for Paul and his family. As most social workers are likely to point out, however, many other significant issues were left unaddressed. How do Mr. and Mrs. R. view the situation and their role in passing on this gene to their son and daughter? Just what does Paul's sister understand about G6PD deficiency? What further steps might the social worker have taken in order to have been a more effective advocate? What steps should be taken to increase the awareness of other military personnel about such screening programs and to change the policies currently in place? Through this one case example, we can see potential implications of genetic screening programs for a number of aspects of social work practice.

Direct involvement in the planning, development, and delivery of genetic screening programs is a natural extension of the functions of public health social work. As the guidelines for genetic screening suggest, careful attention to protection of participants must be built into these programs from the outset. Social workers can lend particular expertise in the development, implementation, and evaluation of informed consent procedures, community education efforts, procedures for communication of test results, and interdisciplinary protocols designed to assure that participants' rights are honored at all stages of the screening process.

Genetic screening programs offer social workers the opportunity to show creative leadership in program development both within the screening programs and in community agencies serving tested populations. Adequate provision of individual counseling and casework services represents only a minimum standard for adequate programs. The frequent implications of genetic diagnoses for nuclear and extended families suggest that priority be given to services that enable family members to come together to discuss concerns and examine the impact of genetic screening on the family unit and on unaffected family members. The social worker can serve as the initial catalyst and leader of support groups that help to lessen the feelings of difference and stigma that newly identified carriers may experience. Such groups, as described in Chapter 5, carry the potential for developing as independent self-help and advocacy groups, which in turn carry the potential for considerable influence on the delivery of genetic screening programs.

Important challenges also exist beyond such direct interventions of program development and clinical services. The dangers as well as the significant public health potential of genetic screening programs call for action by social workers in a range of practice settings:

1. *Advocacy* efforts to challenge discriminatory practices resulting from genetic screening programs and to argue for adequate safeguards in the development and operation of such programs.
2. *Community organizing* efforts to increase citizen awareness of the significance of genetic issues and to foster their involvement in the planning and monitoring of genetic screening laws and programs.
3. *Involvement in legislative and policy-making processes* in order to insure direct social work input into the formulation of new and improved laws and policies to guide future screening efforts. Such efforts might take the form of lobbying, testifying, or even running for public office. The guidelines for genetic screening now available provide a powerful resource for the social worker seeking to influence the development of new policies.
4. *Research* in order to determine the psychosocial impact of various approaches to genetic screening, to identify the variables contributing to the negative aspects of such programs, and to test the efficacy of alternative approaches to service delivery.

Although others might add to or change the focus of this listing, the general implications for social work remain the same. Genetic screening, as a public health effort of increasing significance, demands the involvement of knowledgeable social workers who are prepared to make contributions in a broad range of roles and practice contexts.

NOTE

1. Many of these recommendations have been included in the recent report of the President's Commission for the Study of Ethical Problems in Medicine and Biomedical and Behavioral Research (1983). One of the topics examined by the Presidential Commission was the ethical, social, and legal implications of genetic screening, counseling, and education programs. The small booklet summarizing the Commission's recommendations provides an excellent review of the evolution and status of genetic services and their ethical and legal implications.

Ethical and Legal Issues

Social work has long emphasized its foundation of common values, which, in conjunction with knowledge and skills, define the unique identity of the profession. These primary values emphasize belief in the inherent worth and dignity of the individual and the mutual responsibility individuals hold for each other in meeting the tasks of living. The National Association of Social Workers' (NASW) Code of Ethics (1980) translates these values into certain ethical responsibilities to clients. These include: (1) maintaining a primary responsibility to the client; (2) maximizing the self-determination of clients; (3) respecting the client's right to confidentiality, that is, holding in confidence information obtained in the course of professional services; and (4) promoting the general welfare of society.

Although most social workers readily subscribe in theory to these values and ethical guidelines, their practical application frequently raises dilemmas for social work professionals. Genetic issues and services thus are no different from other areas of social work practice in raising critical questions of values and ethics, and ultimately of the law. Special attention should be given, however, to the specific, and to some degree unique, dilemmas that are emerging with advances in genetic technologies and services. In this chapter we provide an overview of these difficult ethical and legal questions and consider their relationship to social work's values and ethical principles. The issues that we will examine include informed consent, confidentiality, and responsibility to future generations. Our goal is not to provide answers or suggest any definite courses of action; to the contrary, we will attempt to raise issues that will challenge the reader in the spirit expressed so well by Northen (1982):

The practitioner is obliged to take an *informed* [italics added] position on . . . value dilemmas as well as to understand the views of his[her] clients and the organization which employs him[her]. He[she] is faced with the need to make decisions about how to help clients to deal with these dilemmas. A code of ethics reminds him[her] to follow general moral principles, but he[she] is still left with decisions concerning their implementation. (p. 33)

INFORMED CONSENT

The social worker should make every effort to foster maximum self-determination on the part of clients. (NASW Code of Ethics, 1980)

Informed consent reflects one of our highest ethical values—individual autonomy; it implicates strong emotional needs both for control over our own lives and for dependence on others. (Meisel, 1981, p. 198)

Attention to issues involving informed consent is in keeping with the high value that social work places on the maximization of clients' self-determination. Although social workers use the general concept of informed consent as it can apply in a variety of situations arising between clients, professionals, and organizations, in the health field it has taken on a more precise, legal definition:

Informed consent is comprised of two legal duties imposed on physicians—to inform patients about treatment and to obtain their consent for it. These duties are imposed in order to assure that a person's right to self-determination—that is, the right of all free citizens to govern their own destiny—may be maintained in one particular sphere of human activity, the acquisition of medical care. (Meisel, 1981, p. 198)

Traditionally, the duty to disclose medical facts was measured against the standard of the reasonable *physician*. More recently, however, courts have begun to use a yardstick based on the perspective of the *patient*. "What information is material to a reasonable patient who must make a choice?" (Reilly, 1977, p. 165). Doctors still retain some latitude in deciding to withhold certain facts when they view this to be in the patient's best interests, but this right has generally been seen in the context of pre-surgery situations where heightened patient anxiety could complicate critical treatment efforts. Such latitude generally would not apply in genetic counseling situations which rarely involve issues of imminent treatment (Reilly, 1977).

Questions concerning informed consent in genetic services are not resolved, however, by simply accepting the general principle of maximum disclosure on the part of physicians. As social workers would be quick to agree, obtaining truly informed consent requires attention to a complex mix of technical and personal considerations (Meisel, 1981). In all decision making under conditions of uncertainty, informed consent involves the weighing of specific facts and technical information on risks in relation to very personal and subjective values and priorities (Black, 1981; Janis & Mann, 1977). The essential questions that must be answered in determining informed consent are: "To what extent does the person consenting truly *understand* the implications of her/his actions?" and "Under what conditions of freedom and constraint is consent obtained?" (Massarik & Kaback, 1981, p. 132). Informed consent in genetic counseling and testing programs thus may be particularly difficult for clients who face the need to comprehend complex genetic and technical information at a stressful time of heightened anxiety and vulnerability. These problems inevitably will be exacerbated if the system for delivery of genetic services provides little or no time for either thorough review of the technical information or for attention to the personal impact of that material.

Unfortunately, the brief history of genetic services in the United States offers a less than ideal picture of the handling of informed consent. Genetic screening programs have been especially vulnerable to criticism. The early sickle-cell screening programs in particular involved numerous instances in which individuals underwent genetic screening with little or no understanding of either the medical or social implications of the testing. There is little if any disagreement that the scare tactics used in many of the early sickle-cell programs worked in direct contradiction to ethical principles of informed consent. More recently, however, it is becoming apparent that genetic programs must also be evaluated in relation to more subtle criteria. Numerous ambiguities can arise in determining the bases and means for achieving truly informed consent. For example, a Tay-Sachs screening program for 10th- and 11th-grade high school students in Montreal, Canada (Clow & Scriver, 1977) has come under criticism (Holtzman, 1977). Specific questions have been raised regarding the extent of informed consent that can be obtained from high school students. These criticisms have led to even more fundamental concerns about the psychological atmosphere in which consent is sought and the specific information that should be included as a basis for informed consent. As one commentator has argued:

One must . . . question whether consent obtained from the high school students was truly voluntary or informed. The combined effects of an official letter to all Jewish students, a special school assembly, and adolescent peer pressure clearly create a somewhat coercive psychological atmosphere. Although the students were educated about the genetics of TSD, did they know that genetic screening programs were still highly experimental? Were they informed that they were experimental subjects whose participation was in part for the purpose of evaluating the effects of genetic screening programs?

One must wonder whether the students were encouraged to appreciate the rarity of TSD—not only in absolute terms but also in perspective to other far more common genetic and nongenetic preventable birth defects and health problems—or told that only 10 percent of their seniors had agreed to be screened or that the effect of a prior screening of 21,000 Canadian Jews had only prevented one case of TSD—at a cost of $100,000—or that this $100,000 expense siphoned scarce, limited funds from other preventive medical programs concerned with more common and pressing health problems. (Steele, 1981, pp. 356–357)

Turning to another type of genetics program, questions also emerge over the issue of informed consent in relation to prenatal diagnosis. As the volume of demand for this service has increased and the physical risks of the procedure have diminished, many prenatal diagnostic services have begun to develop formats involving much briefer counseling sessions. In some centers most of the information is provided over the telephone or in group sessions. These procedures may provide adequate information for most women to make an informed consent to have the prenatal testing, but systematic evaluations of various approaches will be necessary to determine whether in fact certain groups of women may require more detailed counseling.

Respect for individual autonomy and recognition of the importance of informed decision making have motivated the attention given in recent years to issues of informed consent. Most professionals would agree in principle with these values. As the preceding discussion illustrates, however, ethical dilemmas are raised when one attempts to develop specific procedures for preserving individual autonomy. How does one provide sufficient information about technically complex genetic principles and procedures in a way that maximizes the autonomy of clients rather than adding to their confusion and distress? Where does one draw the line when it comes to specific situations in clinical practice? Particularly in a largely uncharted area such as clinical genetics, who is the expert in saying how much information is enough to insure adequate decision making or at what age young persons should be allowed to assume responsibility for making their own decisions about genetic screening? Social work's professional code of ethics demands active efforts to insure maximum self-determination of clients. This professional mandate implies the need for increased social work involvement not only in considering the general issues of informed consent but also in developing clinical guidelines for addressing the specific situational dilemmas that arise as programs are developed.

CONFIDENTIALITY

The social worker should respect the privacy of clients and hold in confidence all information obtained in the course of professional service. The social worker should share with others confidences revealed by clients, without their consent, only for compelling professional reasons. (NASW Code of Ethics, 1980, pp. 5–6)

Although confidentiality of medical records is a recognized area of general concern, the particular stigmatizing effects of genetic labels and their potential reproductive implications for extended family members have intensified the significance of this issue in genetic services. Precisely because a genetic diagnosis is a "family diagnosis" (Schild, 1977a,b), the boundaries of individual patient confidentiality become blurred, and significant ethical and legal questions emerge. These issues will be considered next in relation to several questions that frequently are raised concerning: (1) disclosures to third parties, such as members of the extended family; (2) discovery of nonpaternity in genetic screening programs; and (3) the potential impact of an increased use of genetic data banks in the future.

Disclosure to Third Parties

The issue of confidentiality, whether between social worker and client or doctor and patient, concerns the individual's right to expect that no information divulged in the course of professional service will be disclosed to a third party without his/her express consent. Social workers are familiar with finding themselves on the boundaries of this ethical principle in situations such as when they are required to report parental statements of potential or actual child abuse, or when they must initiate procedures for involuntary hospitalization of clients. As indicated above, the NASW Code of Ethics acknowledges that "compelling professional reasons" may at times justify selected disclosures without the client's consent. General agreement about just which situations present such compelling reasons is not always easy to reach, and the rather unique dilemmas encountered in genetic services offer a new set of challenges to social workers and other health professionals concerned about preservation of clients' rights to confidentiality.

Social work's recognition that the right to confidentiality has certain limits is reinforced by legal precedents that have shaped the boundaries of confidentiality. The law has come to support the state's right to override the individual's right if it can show substantial counterbalancing interest. More specifically, if there is substantial threat to third parties that may be alleviated by release of information, the state may compel that release (Ball & Omenn, 1980). Clear legal precedent for such practices is widely accepted in the case of infectious diseases, child abuse, and gunshot wounds. Of particular relevance to professionals providing psychological services was the decision in *Tarasoff v Regents of California.* This case involved a situation in which a patient informed his psychologist of his intent to kill his former girlfriend and shortly afterwards committed the murder. The court ruled that the duty of the psychologist to disclose threats of personal harm to the one threatened outweighed the patient's rights of confidentiality in the therapeutic relationship. Social workers now must weigh legal decisions such as this along with other clinical information as they struggle to arrive at the decision on disclosure for each case.

Such questions about the limits of confidentiality have been of particular concern to genetic counselors who may discover that members of the patient's extended family are themselves at risk following a genetic diagnosis in the primary patient. Specific guidance on this question was offered in the final report of the National Academy of Science on genetic screening.

> Under current law, genetic screeners would be ill-advised to contact relatives without the screenee's explicit consent, in view of the sparse case law support for a "public health" exception to the confidentiality rule. (Committee for the Study of Inborn Errors of Metabolism, 1975, p. 186)

The report concluded that a social policy in favor of individual autonomy should have priority over programs aimed at disease reduction. However, as Reilly (1977) has pointed out, this study focused only on mass genetic screening. It did not explicitly address situations arising in the course of work between a private counselor and client. Consider, for example, a case involving a female patient whose son has hemophilia,* an X-linked recessive disorder. What if, following the genetic counseling, the woman refuses to contact her sisters, who are of childbearing age, and will not allow the genetic counselor to warn them of their risks for having affected sons? Even more to the point, what if a social worker in a community agency later sees the woman and becomes aware of this situation? Does that social worker have any responsibility, ethically and/or legally, to pursue actively attempts to get the genetic information to the sisters who unknowingly are at risk for having sons with serious health problems? As clinicians, social workers must weigh their ethical concerns for the rights of these sisters and their unborn children against a primary professional responsibility to their designated client. Stated more generally, does a limited disclosure by a social worker, private physician, or other health professional to a near relative compromise the personal autonomy of the client (Reilly, 1977)? In legal terms, the question becomes: Is there a situation of "imminent danger" for either the close relative who is at risk for producing an affected child or for the unborn child?

Discovery of Nonpaternity

Issues of confidentiality do not necessarily have to involve disclosures to distant third parties. Similarly perplexing dilemmas can arise within the nuclear family when the genetic information suggests questionable paternity of an offspring. Such findings are by no means uncommon, especially in large scale genetic screening programs. Consider the following case situation:

A married couple had what was believed to be a Tay-Sachs* afflicted child in 1974. The child died in the summer of 1976. The couple had come to the genetics clinic to be tested for confirmation of their genetic conditions and for counseling regarding the risk of future offspring with hereditary disease. Analysis of the blood sample of the husband indicates he is not a carrier of Tay-Sachs, but his wife is a carrier.

Under these circumstances:
a. Should the husband be told that he is not a carrier and that his offspring could not be afflicted with Tay-Sachs?
b. If not, should the counselor recommend amniocentesis if the woman becomes pregnant?
c. Based on the choices made in (a) and (b), how should the social worker proceed?

Reilly (1977) has argued that

when a counselor has access to information that could destroy a marriage, he may be justified in withholding it. The usual practice of counselors to inform the woman of the fact situation first makes the most practical sense. (p. 167)

As most mental health professionals are likely to protest, determination of just what information is likely to "destroy a marriage" is in itself a sophisticated professional task requiring in-depth knowledge of the particular family at issue. Moreover, does not withholding of information violate the husband's right to have accurate information on his noncarrier status? This example easily confirms the importance of observing strict standards for genetic screening programs that mandate inclusion of adequate counseling services by qualified mental health professionals.

Genetic Data Banks

As genetic screening programs become more widespread and our ability to determine "genetic vulnerabilities" to certain environments improves, it seems likely that demand will increase for the development of coordinated storage of these genetic data. Access to such centralized data bases could be a powerful tool for public health officials. For example, routine newborn screenings could provide epidemiological data that could serve as an early warning system for teratogens and for tracing subtle correlations between environmental events and multifactorial diseases.

Serious questions regarding protection of the confidentiality of individuals are raised by such plans. Numerous public health statistics currently are compiled through use of anonymous patient records, and similar safeguards could be incorporated into the use of many genetic records. Many other potential uses of genetic data, however, would involve the identification of specific individuals. Possible scenarios (Reilly, 1977) might include a computer scan of genetic records at the time of applications for marriage licenses, jobs, health or life insurance, etc. Such possibilities do not seem unreasonable if one considers that life and health insurance companies already make direct use of genetic data acquired from family histories. Use of more sophisticated genetic screening techniques seems only a logical next step.

Returning to the NASW Code of Ethics (1980), one finds a clear directive linking informed consent to the handling of the preceding situations involving disclosure of confidential information to third parties.

> The social worker should inform clients fully about the limits of confidentiality in a given situation, the purposes for which information is obtained, and how it may be used. (p. 6)

Social workers, if they are to honor their professional Code of Ethics, have an obligation to work toward the inclusion of such protections not only in their own practice but also in the range of genetic services now available. Thus a new element, the program's plans for storing and protecting access to test results, is added to the growing list of information that should be provided to individuals prior to their agreeing to receive genetic screening or counseling services. Threats of legal action only add further strength to this important ethical guideline.

BALANCING RESPONSIBILITIES TO CURRENT AND FUTURE GENERATIONS

We come now to what is perhaps the basic dilemma underlying the preceding concerns about informed consent and confidentiality. What is our personal and professional responsibility to both current and future generations? On this question the NASW Code of Ethics makes no comment. Although the Code of Ethics affirms the social worker's responsibility to promote the general welfare, it remains silent not only about the bases for balancing different levels of need in the current generation but also about the extent to which that responsibility extends to the welfare of future generations. The law becomes similarly vague as we move into this uncharted area.

Taken together, questions of informed consent, confidentiality, and the responsibility to the unborn can be viewed as reflective of three basic goal orientations inherent in genetic counseling: (1) emphasis on the interests and needs of the individual suffering from a genetic disease; (2) emphasis on the interests of parents and especially on their rights to reproductive autonomy; and (3) emphasis on general social benefits (Brunk, 1982). Whose interests should be given priority? For those who seek to mandate newborn screening regardless of parents' wishes, the choice clearly has been made in favor of the rights of the affected infant to treatment. For those who would decide to break from the strict bounds of client/practitioner confidentiality in order to warn relatives of their genetic risks, the greater value again has been placed on the rights of those potentially affected.

But just what decisions are in the best interests of the affected individual or potentially affected individual? There are no ethically clear-cut choices in many genetic situations. Take, for example, the question of the rights of the unborn fetus who is found to carry an extra 21st chromosome (Down syndrome). Responsible individuals, arguing for protection of the rights of that fetus, have reached conclusions both for and against abortion. On the one hand, some argue for the "quality of life" of the affected fetus, concluding that the prospect of mental retardation warrants a decision to terminate the pregnancy. Others look on abortion as a profound violation of the rights of the unborn to life (Wolfensberger, 1981); arguing that no other person can determine whether the life of another individual is worth living.

Questions of reproductive autonomy thus pose particularly thorny dilemmas, because they often fall into the chasm separating individual and societal interests. Conflicts between individual rights of the genetically affected versus the reproductive autonomy of parents are seen played out again over the issue of abortion. Present legal guidelines protect maternal rights to terminate a pregnancy but only up to a certain stage of the pregnancy (*Roe v. Wade,* 1973). After that point, the rights of the fetus or newborn generally take precedence, although even here the current debates over aggressive treatment of defective newborns reflects our society's ambivalent stance on this issue (see, Duff, 1979, 1981; Duff & Campbell, 1975; Fost, 1981; "Reagan warns . . .," 1982). Consideration of general social benefits moves such discussions to an entirely different level, however. It confronts us with the need to move beyond questions of the rights of specific individuals in relation to their families. In other words, should consideration also be given to matters of social priorities and the ultimate limits of an individual's or family's rights?

> Is the right of the individual to reproduce absolute, or may it be limited by other priorities of society? . . . Is the right of the individual to choose to bear or not bear a possibly defective fetus absolute, or is it limited by the consensus of society on abortion? (Steele, 1981, p. 353)

Direct consideration about potential limitations on reproductive autonomy has generally been sidestepped by geneticists and social policy makers. To entertain the notion of actively placing any limits on such rights brings us uncomfortably close to those early goals of eugenics, which served as the initial foundation of genetic counseling. The field of genetic counseling has struggled to disassociate itself from the harmful and misguided efforts of early eugenicists. However, a number of pressures appear to be at work today that are bringing eugenic considerations back into the limelight. As described by Wexler (1980), the first pressure is economic. The costs of caring for the genetically impaired are in the billions of dollars. In these times of scarce resources, society "may well ask why it should continue to absorb these costs when individuals can prevent some of them through abstention from procreation" (Wexler, 1980, p. 315). Insurance companies will hold great power over these decisions in the future as choices are made about whether to provide coverage to the couple who refuses a certain screening test, knowingly undertakes a pregnancy in the face of "high" genetic risks, or refuses to abort a fetus identified by prenatal testing as affected.

The second pressure stems from our increasing ability to screen for hereditary conditions. Each year, as the techniques become simpler and more accessible, genetic screening comes closer to becoming a routine part of general medical and obstetrical care. Such apparent simplicity clearly becomes deceptive when one considers the decisions required when a genetic abnormality is detected.

A third eugenic pressure, noted by Wexler, arises from the increasing availability of alternatives to one's own biological offspring. Offsetting the decline in children available for adoption is the increasing popularity and acceptance of artificial insemination. This procedure presents an important alternative for couples whose parents are carriers of a recessive disease or in which the man carries a gene for a dominant disorder. Rapid progress in techniques for *in vitro* fertilization carry potential for opening up even more options in the near future.

And finally, a fourth eugenic push may develop out of the pressure of children's advocate groups who increasingly have begun to champion the right of every child to be born healthy in mind and body. Recent court cases involving the concept of "wrongful life" provide evidence of this trend. These cases, which have been reviewed in detail elsewhere (see, for example, Damme, 1981; Dowben, 1981; Milunsky & Annas, 1980; Reilly, 1977), bring forward the difficult question of whether it would have been better to have not been born at all than to have been born with a serious defect.

One may choose to view these trends as pressures directing us toward either negative or positive ends. But regardless of which perspective one adopts, it is clear that the choices between the rights of the individual, the family, and society are by no means clear-cut. It seems reasonable to anticipate that individual social workers will draw on their professional and personal values and arrive at different conclusions to these questions. Most important for the preservation of the rights of all parties will be the maintenance of an active, open dialogue about the underlying values and ultimate implications of the choices that will have to be made.

But we are still left with the basic question that introduces this section: What is the proper balance of responsibilities to current and future generations? Daniel Callahan (1973), a noted ethicist, has eloquently captured this dilemma:

> How can we manage both to live humanely with genetic disease and yet to conquer it at the same time? Both goals seem imperative and yet the logic of each is different. We cure disease by ceasing to romanticize it, by gathering our powers to attack it, by making it an enemy to be conquered. We learn to live with a disease, however, in a very different way; by trying to accept and cherish those who manifest the disease, by shaping social structures and institutions that will soften the individual suffering brought on by the disease, by refusing to make the bearer of the disease our economic, social or political enemy.
>
> Our communal task, I believe, is to find a way of combining both logics. . . . It will mean, for instance, simultaneously working to improve the social treatment and respect accorded those born with defects, and working to extend our genetic knowledge and applying it to genetic counseling. It will mean taking the idea of free choice seriously, allowing parents to make their own choice without penalizing them socially for the choices they make, or condemning them for those choices which will increase the financial costs to society. Part of the very meaning of human continuity, I would contend, entails a willingness of society to bear the social costs of individual freedom. (p. 89)

The mandate for social work can be seen in the above statement. As a profession, social work has actively committed itself to maximizing the self-determination and autonomy of clients and to developing policies and programs that will serve as wise and humane investments for enhancing the public's well-being. It is now the responsibility of social work to take on a new challenge: to enhance the well-being of future generations without, at the same time, compromising the rights and well-being of the current generation.

Epilogue: Future Challenges

We have identified the clear relevance of the connection between social work and genetics and demonstrated that social workers in many areas of practice have important contributions to make in work with people facing genetic concerns. We have delineated the knowledge base for practice that already exists, albeit in a beginning stage of development. The question that naturally comes to mind is what now for social work in genetics? What tasks remain and what challenges should be met?

The most urgent task facing the profession is preparing social workers for effective practice in genetics. Detailed recommendations for training efforts in graduate and continuing education have been developed (Forsman & Bishop, 1981) and innovative programs are underway (Black, 1982).

It will be difficult to maintain this forward momentum in the face of shrinking resources and competing needs. However, the rapid pace of genetic advances and proliferation of clinical genetic services should challenge the profession to prepare its practitioners to assume leadership roles in the planning and delivery of these services. The 21st century is close upon us, and we need to heed the signals that point toward what may be expected in living in an even more technological society.

A second task of importance is to expand the knowledge base underpinning practice in genetics. The social work literature, which in October 1969 contained only four articles dealing specifically with social work and genetics, has grown significantly in the past 15 years. Social work writers have documented their increasing involvement in genetic issues and have begun to articulate some of the dynamics of practice with genetic concerns. It is imperative that social work reporting and investigations continue. We need to learn as much as possible about clients as they express genetic concerns in all aspects of their lives. This kind of psychosocial research provides social work with the opportunity to enhance its credibility as a valued partner in the provision of genetic services and to contribute valuable knowledge for use by all professionals involved in delivering genetic services. Of particular importance will be research conducted in fields of practice outside the health area. We have only begun to identify the implications of genetic issues for the fields of adoptions and mental health. A more sophisticated understanding of genetic disorders also will be needed by school social workers as more and more disabled children are mainstreamed into the public schools. At the same time, school social workers will have the opportunity to study and to contribute new understandings of the impact of genetic disorders on developing children and their families. Similarly, social workers in industrial settings will be in the forefront in defining and addressing genetic issues in the workplace.

Yes, we have much to learn; *yet we already have much to offer.* The challenges of the future should not prevent us from affirming loudly the contributions we can make now with our current knowledge and skills in social work practice.

Glossary

alleles. Alternative forms of a gene that occupy identical sites on homologous chromosomes and that determine alternative characteristics in inheritance.

amniocentesis. A method of prenatal diagnosis that involves withdrawal of a small amount of amniotic fluid from the amniotic sac; the fluid surrounds the fetus and contains cells from the fetal membranes or shed by the fetus.

autosome. Any of the 44 (22 pair) nonsex chromosomes.

carrier. An individual who possesses a recessive gene together with its normal allele. Although the recessive gene is not expressed, the individual can transmit the gene to progeny who would express it if another recessive gene at the same site is inherited from the other parent. The term is also used for the presymptomatic or asymptomatic state of an individual who carries an autosomal dominant gene.

chorionic villi. The tissue that surrounds the developing embryo in the first weeks of pregnancy and forms the placenta and fetal membranes. These villi are obtained by suction biopsy through the cervix to provide prenatal diagnoses in the first trimester of pregnancy.

chromosome. A cigar-shaped structure containing DNA that is located in the cell nucleus. The number of chromosomes is characteristic for a given species; the normal number in humans is 46, with 22 pairs of autosomes and 2 sex chromosomes (XX or XY).

congenital. Present at birth.

cytogenetics. The study of the structure and function of chromosomes.

deletion. Loss of part of a chromosome that results in an imbalance of genetic material.

DNA (deoxyribonucleic acid). A nucleic acid found in all living cells that comprises the genetic material in chromosomes. Every inherited characteristic has its origin somewhere in the code of each individual's complement of DNA.

dominant gene. A gene that is expressed in a single copy (or in the heterozygous state). An autosomal or X-linked dominant disease is caused by such a gene.

dysmorphism. Developmental abnormality of the form and structure of an individual. (adjective: dysmorphic)

empiric risk. Estimate that a trait will occur or recur in a family based on past experience rather than on knowledge of the causative mechanism.

eugenics. The study of methods to improve the hereditary constitution of a species.

fetoscopy. A procedure that permits direct visualization of the fetus and the placenta through a device that is put through a hollow needle inserted through the abdominal wall into the uterus and amniotic sac.

gamete. A male or female reproductive cell (i.e., the sperm or the egg) whose union is necessary in sexual reproduction to initiate the development of a new individual. Gametes differ from other cells in that they contain only half the usual number of chromosomes.

gene. The basic unit of heredity. It is made up of DNA and located in a definite position on a particular chromosome.

genotype. The genetic constitution of an individual, including alleles that are not expressed.

heterozygote. An individual possessing a variant gene and a normal gene at identical sites of homologous chromosomes. (adjective: heterozygous)

homologous chromosomes. A "matched pair" of chromosomes, one from each parent, having the same gene loci in the same order.

homozygote. An individual possessing an identical pair of alleles, either both normal or both variant, at identical sites of homologous chromosomes. (adjective: homozygous)

inversion. A reversal of the usual gene order along a segment of a chromosome.

karyotype. The chromosome set. The term is often used for a photomicrograph of the chromosomes of an individual, arranged in the standard classification, or as a verb to indicate the process of preparing such a photomicrograph.

linkage. Linked genes have their loci within measurable genetic distance of one another on the same chromosome. The closer they are to each other on the chromosome, the more often they are transmitted together.

locus. The position that a gene occupies on a chromosome.

meiosis. A type of cell division that occurs only in the germ cells during the formulation of gametes in sexually reproducing organisms. Two consecutive cell divisions occur but only one division of the chromosome occurs, thus the number of chromosomes in the gametes is reduced by half.

mitosis. A type of cell division in which the chromosome set of the resultant cells (daughter cells) is identical to that of the parent cell. Mitosis is characteristic of somatic cells and of germ cells before the onset of meiosis.

monosomy. The absence of one member of a chromosome pair.

mosaic. An individual or tissue with at least two cell lines differing in genotype or karyotype, derived from a single fertilized egg.

multifactorial. Traits determined by interaction of multiple gene pairs with environmental factors.

mutation. A structural alteration in the DNA of a gene resulting in a permanent, transmissible change in the genetic makeup of an individual such that the characteristics of an offspring are different from those of his or her parents. A mutation is usually defined as a change in a single gene (point mutation), although the term is sometimes used more broadly to describe a structural chromosomal change.

nondisjunction. The failure of paired chromosomes to separate during meiosis or mitosis.

pedigree. In medical genetics, a diagrammatic representation of a family history (a family tree), indicating the affected individuals and their relationship to the propositus (proband).

penetrance. When the frequency of expression of a genotype is less than 100%, the trait is said to exhibit reduced penetrance. In an individual who has a genotype that characteristically produces an abnormal phenotype but who is phenotypically normal, the trait is said to be nonpenetrant.

phenotype. The entire expressed physical, biochemical, and physiological constitution of an individual.

proband. See *propositus.*

propositus. The family member who first draws attention to a pedigree of a given trait. Also called *index case* or *proband.*

recessive gene. A gene that is *not* expressed in a single copy (or in the heterozygous state). A recessive disease is caused by two copies (or homozygous state) of such a gene in autosomal disorders or one copy on a male's X chromosome in X-linked disorders.

sex chromosome. Chromosomes responsible for sex determination, i.e., the X or the Y chromosome. Normal human males have one X and one Y (XY); normal human females have two Xs (XX).

syndrome. The set of signs and symptoms characteristic of a specific disorder.

teratogen. An agent (such as certain drugs) that produces or raises the incidence of congenital malformations.

trait. A characteristic or phenotype. The word is sometimes used to designate a heterozygous carrier; for example, sickle cell trait refers to a healthy carrier.

translocation. An error occurring during chromosomal replication, whereby a chromosome or a fragment of it becomes attached to another chromosome.

trisomy. The presence of a third chromosome in cells that normally contain two, as in trisomy 21 (Down syndrome).

variable expressivity. Refers to the sometimes wide range of phenotypes that can result in different individuals who have the same genotype.

Selected Review of Genetic Disorders

Disorders included in this listing have been identified in the text with an (*).

Adrenoleukodystrophy (ALD). X-linked recessive disorder involving the adrenal glands and the white matter of the brain and peripheral nervous system; results in progressive paralysis with spasticity and adrenal insufficiency.

Apert syndrome. Autosomal dominant; characterized by abnormal fusion of the sutures of the skull, a flat facial appearance; syndactyly (webbing of the fingers), and occasionally mental retardation.

cystic fibrosis. Autosomal recessive; a condition involving abnormalities in secretions of certain digestive enzymes, salts in sweat, and bronchial secretions; thick, viscid mucous produced by the bronchi make affected children highly susceptible to pneumonia; males generally are infertile as a secondary consequence of abnormal mucous secretions in the vas deferens; loss of salts in the sweat may be severe enough to cause heat prostration in warm weather.

Down syndrome. Chromosome disorder involving triplication of the 21st chromosome; frequent characteristics include mental retardation, decreased muscle tone (hypotonia), flat occiput, epicanthal folds at the eyes, low nasal bridge, simian or single transverse crease of the palm, and shortened stature; karyotype indicates trisomy 21 (95% of cases), a translocation (4%), or mosaicism (1%).

G6PD (glucose 6-phosphate dehydrogenase) deficiency. X-linked recessive; involves a defect in the enzyme G6PD; affected individuals are at risk for developing hemolytic anemia when exposed to certain foods and drugs, such as antimalarial agents, but are otherwise healthy; some carrier females may show symptoms.

hemophilia. X-linked recessive for hemophilia A and B; a disorder of blood clotting in which activity of a blood plasma protein or factor necessary for clotting is deficient; the most common variety is called hemophilia A or classical hemophilia and results from a deficiency of factor VIII; the next most common type is hemophilia B or Christmas disease and involves factor IX; the severity of the clotting problem differs greatly among individuals.

Huntington disease. Autosomal dominant; a progressive, neurological disorder with onset usually in midadult life; associated with gradual development of involuntary movements, intellectual decline, and psychiatric difficulties.

Klinefelter syndrome (XXY). A chromosome disorder involving an extra copy of the X sex chromosome; characterized by tall stature; small testes and penis, usually accompanied by sterility; feminine characteristics such as breast development and sparse facial and sexual hair, and increased risk of mental retardation.

Marfan syndrome. Autosomal dominant, tall stature, long, slim limbs, hyperextensibility of joints, eye and cardiovascular problems, shortened life span due to cardiovascular difficulties, with average age of death in mid-40s.

neurofibromatosis. Autosomal dominant with wide variability in severity of expression; characterized by multiple cafe-au-lait spots on the skin and tumors, which may be widespread and result in a range of difficulties.

osteogenesis imperfecta. A term applied to a heterogeneous group of disorders characterized by increased bone fragility; autosomal dominant and recessive forms have been identified; the three main signs are brittle bones, blue sclerae (white part of eye), and deafness from otosclerosis (bony abnormalities in the middle and inner ear); highly variable in expression, some severely affected children may have multiple fractures at birth and be stillborn, in others the expression may be so mild that the diagnosis is never made.

phenylketonuria (PKU). Autosomal recessive; metabolic disorder that results in severe mental retardation if left untreated; detectable in the newborn period by screening tests and treatable with special diet.

progeria. Uncertain etiology; exceedingly rare disorder with precocious aging of striking degree; early death usually results from progressive coronary artery disease; average life span 14 years; normal intelligence.

Schwartz-Jampel syndrome. Autosomal recessive; progressive myotonia (increased muscular irritability and contractility with decreased power of relaxation) and muscle wasting resulting in joint limitation; small stature; sad, fixed facial appearance.

sickle cell disease. Autosomal recessive; a blood disorder characterized by the tendency of the red cells to become abnormal in shape, i.e., "sickled cells," under conditions of low oxygen; symptoms include anemia, jaundice, and painful "sickle cell crises" caused when sickled cells clog in the vessels and cut off blood flow to various parts of the body; heterozygous carriers are usually clinically normal; occurs most frequently in people originating from equatorial Africa, less commonly from the Mediterranean, Arabia, and India.

Tay-Sachs disease. Autosomal recessive; a progressive, neurological disorder; in the U.S. primarily found among Ashkenazi Jews; onset in early infancy with decline in functioning leading to death usually in a few years.

the thalassemias. Autosomal recessive for the major forms; these are a group of disorders resulting from a reduced rate of synthesis of either of the molecular chains that make up hemoglobin; they occur in two forms: a severe form, thalassemia major (homozygous) and a mild form, thalassemia minor (heterozygous, or in some cases homozygous for a milder defect); the thalassemias are found more frequently in peoples from the Mediterranean and Middle East, and parts of Africa, India, and the Orient.

Treacher Collins syndrome. Autosomal dominant (60% of cases may represent new mutations); most frequent features include under development of cheek bones and lower jaw; malformation of external ear; absence of a small part of lower eyelid; and conductive hearing loss (in 40% of cases).

trichorhinophalangeal syndrome. Autosomal dominant; associated with small stature; sparse, slow-growing hair; bulbous, pear-shaped nose; deformity of joints; progressive arthritic symptoms of dorsal spine and fingers.

tuberous sclerosis. Autosomal dominant (86% of cases may represent new mutations); wide variation in severity; in its full expression, characterized by skin nodules, seizures, retinal tumors, bone lesions, and mental deficiency; white, leaf-shaped spots on the skin, present from birth, are often useful in diagnosis of otherwise unaffected individuals.

Turner syndrome (45,XO). Chromosome disorder involving presence of only a single sex chromosome, an X chromosome; characterized by sterility, short stature, webbing of the neck and cubitus valgus (increased carrying angle of the elbow); other health problems can include orthopedic, kidney, and heart defects.

References and Selected Bibliography

Abelson, R. P. (1976). Script processing in attitude formation and decision making. In J. S. Carroll & J. W. Payne (Eds.), *Cognition and social behavior*. Hillsdale, NJ: Lawrence Erlbaum.

Adams, M. M., Finley, S., Hansen, H., Jahiel, R., Oakley, G., Sanger, W., Wells, G., & Wertelecki, W. (1981). Utilization of prenatal genetic diagnosis in women 35 years of age and older in the United States, 1977 to 1978. *American Journal of Obstetrics and Gynecology, 139*, 673-677.

Antley, M. A., Antley, R. M., & Hartlage, L. C. (1973). Effects of genetic counseling on parental self-concepts. *Journal of Psychology, 83*, 335-338.

Antley, R. M. (1976, Summer). Variables in the outcome of genetic counseling. *Social Biology, 23*, 108-115.

Antley, R. M., Hartlage, L. C., & Kopetzke, C. A. (1972). Factors related to and responding to genetic counseling. *American Journal of Human Genetics, 24*, 27a.

Ashery, R. S. (1977). Prenatal diagnosis: Is amniocentesis a crisis situation? In W. T. Hall & C. L. Young (Eds.), *Proceedings—Genetic disorders: Social service interventions*. Conference sponsored by the Graduate School of Public Health, University of Pittsburgh, and the Office for Maternal and Child Health, DHHS, PHS, BCHS, pp. 40-48.

Ball, J. R., & Omenn, G. S. (1980). Genetics, adoption, and the laws. In A. Milunsky & G. Annas (Eds.), *Genetics and the law II*. New York: Plenum Press.

Bartlett, H. (1961). *Social work practice in the health field*. Washington, DC: National Association of Social Workers.

Becker, R. S. (1973). *Outsiders: Studies in the sociology of deviance* (2nd ed.). New York: Free Press.

Beeson, D., & Golbus, M. (1979) Anxiety engendered by amniocentesis. *Birth Defects Original Article Series, 15*(5c). New York: Liss, pp. 191-197.

Bessman, S. P., & Swazey, J. P. (1971). Phenylketonuria: A study of biomedical legislation. In E. Mendelsohn, J. P. Swazey, & I. Taviss (Eds.), *Human aspects of biomedical innovation*. Cambridge, MA: Harvard University Press.

Black, R. B. (1978). *Coping with risks under conditions of varying uncertainty*. Unpublished doctoral dissertation. University of California, Berkeley.

Black, R. B. (1979). The effects of diagnostic uncertainty and available options on perceptions of risk. *Birth Defects Original Article Series, 15*(5c). New York: Liss, pp. 341-354.

Black, R. B. (1980a). Parents' evaluations of genetic counseling. *Patient Counselling and Health Education, 2*, 142-146.

Black, R. B. (1980b). Support for genetic services: A survey. *Health and Social Work, 5*, 27-34.

Black, R. B. (1981). Risk-taking behavior: Decision making in the face of genetic uncertainty. *Social Work in Health Care, 7*, 11-25.

Black, R. B. (1982). Social work trends: Education in genetics for social workers moves beyond the basics. In D. Brantley & S. Wright (Eds.), *Coordinating comprehensive child health services: Service, training, and applied research perspectives*. Based on the proceedings of the 1981 Tri-Regional Workshop for Social Workers in Maternal and Child Health Services. Sponsored by Center for Developmental and Learning Disorders, University of Alabama in Birmingham and Office for Maternal and Child Health, Bureau of Community Health Services, Health Services Administration, Public Health Service, USDHHS.

Black, R. B. (1983). Genetics and adoption: A challenge for social work. In M. Dinerman (Ed.), *Social work practice in a turbulent world*. Silver Spring, MD: National Association of Social Workers.

Blumberg, B., Golbus, M., & Hanson, K. (1975). The psychological sequelae of abortion performed for a genetic indication. *American Journal of Obstetrics and Gynecology, 122*, 799-808.

Boehm, C. D., Antonarakis, S. E., Stylianos, E. A., Phillips, J. A., Stetten, G., & Kazazian, H. H. (1983). Prenatal diagnosis using DNA polymorphisms. *New England Journal of Medicine, 308*, 1054-1058.

Bracht, N. F. (1978). *Social work in health care: A guide to professional practice*. New York: Haworth Press.

*Brantley, D. (1980). A genetics primer for social workers. *Health and Social Work, 5*, 5-13.
*Bregman, A. M. (1980). Living with progressive childhood illness: Parental management of neuromuscular disease. *Social Work in Health Care, 5*, 387-408.
Brunk, C. (1982). Genetic counseling. In S. A. Yelaja (Ed.), *Ethical issues in social work*. Springfield, IL: Charles C Thomas.
Callahan, D. (1973). The meaning and significance of genetic disease: Philosophical perspectives. In B. Hilton, D. Callahan, M. Harris, P. Condliffe, & B. Berkley (Eds.), *Ethical issues in human genetics*. New York: Plenum Press.
Carr, D. N. (1967). Chromosome anomalies as a cause of spontaneous abortions. *American Journal of Obstetrics and Gynecology, 97*, 283-293.
Check, W. A. (1980). Genetic counseling—Still mostly genetics. *Journal of the American Medical Association, 244*, 315-317.
Childs, B., Gordis, L., Kaback, M. M., & Kazazian, A. (1976). Tay-Sachs screening: Social and psychological impact. *American Journal of Human Genetics, 28*, 550-558.
Cohen, J. (1980). Nature of clinical social work. In P. L. Ewalt (Ed.), *Toward a definition of clinical social work*. Washington, DC: National Association of Social Workers.
Clow, C. L., & Scriver, C. R. (1977). Knowledge about and attitudes toward screening among high-school students: The Tay-Sachs experience. *Pediatrics, 59*, 85-91.
Collins, A. H., & Pancoast, D. L. (1976). *Natural helping networks: A strategy for prevention*. Washington, DC: National Association of Social Workers.
Committee for the Study of Inborn Errors of Metabolism. (1975). *Genetic screening: Programs, principles, and research*. Washington, DC: National Academy of Science.
Conyard, S., Krishnamurthy, M., & Dosik, H. (1980). Psychosocial aspects of sickle-cell anemia in adolescents. *Health and Social Work, 5*, 20-26.
Damme, C. (1981). Medicolegal aspects of genetics: Standards of care. In S. R. Applewhite, D. L. Busbee, & D. S. Borgaonkar (Eds.), *Genetic screening and counseling: A multidisciplinary perspective*. Springfield, IL: Charles C Thomas.
Daniels, L., & Berg, G. M. (1968). The crisis of birth and adaptive patterns of amputee children. *Clinical Proceedings of Children's Hospitals DC, 24*, 108-117.
Dowben, C. (1981). Legal considerations in prenatal care. In S. R. Applewhite, D. L. Busbee, & D. S. Borgaonkar (Eds.), *Genetic screening and counseling: A multidisciplinary perspective*. Springfield, IL: Charles C Thomas.
Drotar, D., Baskiewicz, A., Irvin, N., Kennell, J. H., & Klaus, M. H. (1975). The adaptation of parents to the death of an infant with congenital malformation: A hypothetical model. *Pediatrics, 56*, 710-717.
Duff, R. S. Guidelines for deciding care of critically ill or dying patients. *Pediatrics, 1979, 64*, 17-23.
Duff, R. S. (1981). Counseling families and deciding care of severely defective children: A way of coping with "medical Vietnam." *Pediatrics, 67*, 315-320.
Duff, R. S., & Campbell, A. G. M. (1975). Moral and ethical dilemmas in the special care nursery. *New England Journal of Medicine, 289*, 890-894.
Epstein, C. J. (1974). Genetic counseling—Past, present, and future. In K. D. Moghissi (Ed.), *Birth defects and fetal development: Endocrine and metabolic factors*. Springfield, IL: Charles C Thomas.
Epstein, C. J. (1975). Genetic counseling: Present status and future prospects. In L. N. Went, C. Vermeij-Keers, and & A. G. J. M. vander Linden (Eds.), *Early diagnosis and prevention of genetic diseases*. Leiden: Leiden University Press.
Epstein, C. J., Erickson, R. P., Hall, B. D., & Golbus, M. S. (1975). The center satellite system for wide-scale distribution of genetic counseling services. *American Journal of Human Genetics, 27*, 322-332.
Ewalt, P. (Ed.). (1980). *Toward a definition of clinical social work*. Washington, DC: National Association of Social Workers.
Featherstone, H. (1980). *A difference in the family*. New York: Penguin Books. 1980.
Fletcher, J. (1972). The brink: The parent-child bond in the genetic revolution. *Theological Studies, 33*, 457-485.

(*) Indicates additional references relevant to social work and genetics not cited elsewhere in this volume.

Fletcher, J. (1973). Parents in genetic counseling: The moral shape of decision making. In B. Hilton, D. Callahan, M. Harris, P. Condliffe, and B. Berkley (Eds.), *Ethical issues in human genetics.* New York: Plenum Press.

Forsman, I., & Bishop, K. K. (Eds.). (1981). *Education in genetics: Nurses and social workers.* DHHS Pub. No. (HSA) 81-5120A.

Fost, N. (1981). Counseling families who have a child with a severe congenital anomaly. *Pediatrics, 67,* 321-324.

Fox, G. L. (Ed.). (1982). *The childbearing decision—Fertility attitudes and behavior.* Beverly Hills, CA: Sage Publications.

Fraser, F. C. (1963). On being a medical geneticist. *American Journal of Human Genetics, 15,* 1-10.

Fraser, F. C. (1974). Genetic counseling. *American Journal of Human Genetics, 26,* 636-659.

Fraser, F. C., & Levy, E. P. (1972). Follow-up of a genetic counseling program. *American Journal of Human Genetics, 24,* 30a.

Fuchs, F. (1980). Genetic amniocentesis. *Scientific American, 242,* 47-53.

Gartner, A., & Riessman, F. (1977). *Self help in the human services.* San Francisco: Jossey-Bass.

Germain, C. (Ed.). (1979). *Social work practice—People and environments: An ecological perspective.* New York: Columbia University Press.

Golan, N. (1978). *Treatment in crisis situations.* New York: Free Press.

Golden, D., Davis, J., & Leary, L. (1981). The contribution of long-term psychosocial services to the genetic counseling process. In S. A. Applewhite, D. L. Busbee, & D. S. Borgaonkar (Eds.), *Genetic screening and counseling: A multidisciplinary perspective.* Springfield, IL: Charles C Thomas.

Goodman, M. J., & Goodman, L. E. (1982). The overselling of genetic anxiety. *Hastings Center Report, 12,* 20-27.

Griffin, M. L., Kavanagh, C. M., & Sorenson, J. R. (1976). Genetic knowledge, client perspectives, and genetic counseling. *Social Work in Health Care, 2,* 171-180.

Guerin, P. J., & Pendagast, E. G. (1976). Evaluation of family system and genogram. In P. T. Guerin (Ed.), *Family therapy: Theory and practice.* New York: Halsted Press.

Hall, W. T., & Young, C. L. (Eds.). (1977). *Proceedings: Genetic disorders. Social service interventions.* Conference sponsored by the Graduate School of Public Health, University of Pittsburgh, and the Office for Maternal and Child Health, DHHS, PHS, BCHS.

Hamerton, J. (1971). Cytogenetics of human pregnancy wastage. In J. Hamerton (Ed.), *Human cytogenetics,* vol. II. New York: Academic Press.

Hamilton, D. L. (1976). Cognitive biases in the perception of social groups. In J. S. Carroll & J. W. Payne (Eds.), *Cognition and social behavior.* Hillsdale, NJ: Lawrence Erlbaum.

Hartman, A. (1978). Diagrammatic assessment of family relationships. *Social Casework, 59,* 465-476.

Hecht, F., & Holmes, L. B. (1972). What we don't know about genetic counseling. *New England Journal of Medicine, 287,* 464.

Henig, R. M. (1982, February 28). Saving babies before birth. *The New York Times Magazine.*

Holtzman, N. A. (1977). *Genetic screening for better or for worse? Pediatrics, 59,* 131-133.

Hook, E. B. (1980). Genetic counseling dilemmas: Down syndrome, paternal age, and recurrence risk after remarriage. *American Journal of Medical Genetics, 5,* 145-151.

Hook, E. B., & Chambers, G. M. (1977). Estimated rates of Down's syndrome in live births by one year maternal age intervals for mothers aged 20-49 in a New York State study. *Birth Defects Original Article Series, 13*(3A). New York: Liss, pp. 123-141.

Hook, E. B., Cross, P. K., & Schreinemachers, D. M. (1982, September-October). Contemporary estimates of maternal age specific rates of Down's syndrome and trisomies in live-births (in absence of selective abortions) using regression smoothed rates from prenatal diagnosis studies adjusted for spontaneous fetal death after amniocentesis. Presented at the 1982 Annual Meeting, American Society of Human Genetics, Detroit.

Hook, E. B., Schreinemachers, D. M., & Cross, P. (1981). Use of prenatal cytogenetic diagnosis in New York State. *New England Journal of Medicine, 305,* 1410-1413.

Janis, I. L., & Mann, L. (1977). *Decision making.* New York: Free Press.

Johns, M. (1971). Family reactions to the birth of a child with a congenital abnormality. *Medical Journal of Australia, 1,* 277-282.

Kaback, M. M. (Ed.). (1977). *Tay-Sachs disease: Screening and prevention.* New York: Liss.

Kamin, L. J. (1974). The science and politics of IQ. Hillsdale, NJ: Lawrence Erlbaum.

Karp, L. E. (1980). Editorial comment on Dr. Hook's paper. *American Journal of Medical Genetics, 5*, 153–155.

Katz, A. H. (1980). Genetic counseling in chronic disease. *Health and Social Work, 5*, 14–19.

Katz, A. H., & Bender, E. I. (Eds.). (1976). *The strength in us: Self help groups in the modern world.* New York: New Viewpoints.

Kenen, R. H., & Schmidt, R. M. (1978). Stigmatization of carrier status: Social implications of heterozygote genetic screening programs. *American Journal of Public Health, 68*, 1116–1120.

Kessler, S. (Ed.). (1979). *Genetic counseling: Psychological dimensions.* New York: Academic Press.

Kiely, L., Sterne, R., & Witkop, C. J. (1976). Psychological factors in low-incidence genetic disease: The case of osteogenesis imperfecta. *Social Work in Health Care, 1*(4), 409–420.

Kolata, G. B. (1980). Prenatal diagnosis of neural tube defects. *Science, 209*, 1216–1218.

Kramm, E. R. (1963). *Families of Mongoloid children.* Washington, DC: U.S. Dept. Health, Education, and Welfare. Children's Bureau Publication No. 401.

Krush, A. (1981). Social work role in research studies of families having hereditary cancer and precancer diagnoses. *Social Work in Health Care, 7*(2), 39–48.

Lazarus, R. S. (1966). *Psychological stress and the coping process.* New York: McGraw-Hill.

Lemert, E. M. (1951). *Social pathology.* New York: McGraw-Hill.

Leonard, C. O., Chase, G. A., & Childs, B. (1972). Genetic counseling: A consumer's view. *New England Journal of Medicine, 287*, 433–439.

LePontois, J. (1975). Adolescents with sickle cell anemia deal with life and death. *Social Work in Health Care, 1*(1), 71–80.

Lieberman, M. A., & Borman, L. D. (Eds.). (1979). *Self help groups for coping with crisis.* San Francisco: Jossey-Bass.

Lippman-Hand, A., & Fraser, F. C. (1979a). Genetic counseling: Parents' responses to uncertainty. *Birth Defects Original Article Series, 15*(5c). New York: Liss, pp. 325–339.

Lippman-Hand, A., & Fraser, F. C. (1979b). Genetic counseling: Provision and reception of information. *American Journal of Medical Genetics, 3*, 113–127.

Lippman-Hand, A., & Fraser, F. C. (1979c). Genetic counseling—The postcounseling period: I. Parents' perceptions of uncertainty. *American Journal of Medical Genetics, 4*, 51–71.

Lippman-Hand, A., & Fraser, F. C. (1979d). Genetic counseling—The post-counseling period: II. Making reproductive choices. *American Journal of Medical Genetics, 4*, 73–87.

Loehlin, J., Lindzey, G., & Spuhler, J. (1975). *Race differences in intelligence.* San Francisco: W. H. Freeman.

Lowenberg, F., & Dolgoff, R. (1982). *Ethical considerations in social work practice.* Itasca, IL: F. E. Peacock.

Louro, J. M. (1981). Genetics and birth defects. In S. R. Applewhite, D. L. Busbee, & D. S. Borgaonkar (Eds.), *Genetic screening and counseling: A multidisciplinary perspective.* Springfield, IL: Charles C Thomas.

Lubs, H., & delaCruz, F. (1977). *Genetic counseling.* New York: Raven Press.

Ludmerer, K. M. (1972). *Genetics and American society: A historical appraisal.* Baltimore: Johns Hopkins University Press.

Lynch, H. T., Fain, P., & Marrero, K. (1980). *International directory of genetic services* (6th ed). White Plains, NY: March of Dimes Birth Defects Foundation.

Marion, J. P., Kassam, G., Farnhoff, P. M., Brantley, K. E., Carroll, L., Zacharias, J., Klein, L., Priest, J. H., & Elsas, L. G. (1980). Acceptance of amniocentesis by low-income patients in an urban hospital. *American Journal of Obstetrics and Gynecology, 138*, 11–15.

Massarik, F., & Kaback, M. M. (1981). *Genetic disease control: A social psychological approach.* Beverly Hills: Sage Publications.

McGrath, F. C., & Owen, R. (1975). *Survey: Genetics and genetic counseling in social work education.* Miami: Division of Social Work, University of Miami Mailman Center for Child Development.

McKusick, V. A. (1983). *Mendelian inheritance in man* (6th ed.). Baltimore: Johns Hopkins University Press.

Meisel, A. (1981). Informed consent—Who decides for whom? In M. D. Hiller (Ed.), *Medical ethics and the law.* Cambridge, MA: Ballinger.

Meyer, C. (1976). *Social work practice—The changing landscape* (2nd ed.). New York: Free Press.

Miller, E. (1976). The social work component in community-based action on behalf of victims of Huntington's disease. *Social Work in Health Care. 2*, 25-32.

Milunsky, A. (1975). *The prevention of genetic disease and mental retardation*. Philadelphia: W.B. Saunders.

Milunsky, A. (1977). *Know your genes*. New York: Avon Books.

Milunsky, A., & Annas, G. J. (1980). *Genetics and the law II*. New York: Plenum Press.

Money, J., Klein, A., & Beck, J. (1979). Counseling and psychotherapy in sex-chromosome disorders. In S. Kessler (Ed.), *Genetic counseling: Psychological dimensions*. New York: Academic Press.

Morris, H., & Hirsch, N. (1982). *Support groups for Huntington's disease families*. National Huntington's Disease Association, 1182 Broadway, Suite 402, New York, NY 10001.

*Murray, R. F. (1976). Psychological aspects of genetic counseling. *Social Work in Health Care. 2*, 13-24.

National Association of Social Workers. (1980). *Code of Ethics*. Washington, DC: National Association of Social Workers.

Nesser, W. S., & Sudderth, G. B. (1965). Genetics and casework. *Social Casework, 46*, 22-25.

NICHD Study Group. (1976). Midtrimester amniocentesis for prenatal diagnosis: Safety and accuracy. *Journal of American Medical Association, 236*, 1471-1476.

Noel, B., & Revil, D. (1974). Some personality perspectives of XYY individuals taken from the general population. *Journal of Sex Research, 10*, 219-225.

Northen, H. (1982). *Clinical social work*. New York: Columbia University Press.

Olshansky, S. (1962). Chronic sorrow: A response to having a mentally retarded child. *Social Casework, 43*, 190-193.

*Oppenheimer, J. R., & Rucker, R. W. (1980). The effect of parental relationships on the management of cystic fibrosis and guidelines for social work intervention. *Social Work in Health Care, 5*, 409-419.

Panides, W. (1979). Coping mechanisms and resource management: Implications for social work practice. In I. S. Zemzars & R. A. Ritvo (Eds.), *Perinatology. The role of social work in practice, research, and professional education*. Proceedings, conference sponsored by Office for Maternal and Child Health (DHHS, PHS, BCHS) and School of Applied Social Sciences, Case Western Reserve University, Cleveland, Ohio.

Plumridge, D. (1976). *Good things come in small packages. The whys and hows of Turners syndrome*. Portland, OR: Crippled Children's Division, The Oregon Health Sciences University.

Plumridge, D. (1980). *Autosomal chromosomal abnormality: A cause of birth defects*. Portland, OR: Crippled Children's Division, The Oregon Health Sciences University.

Plumridge, D., Barkost, C. P., & LaFranchi, S. (1982). *Klinefelter syndrome. The X-tra special boy and for boys only*. Portland, OR: Crippled Children's Division, The Oregon Health Sciences University.

Pohlman, E. (1969). *The psychology of birth planning*. Cambridge, MA: Schenkman.

Powledge, T. (1974). Genetic screening as a political and social development. *Birth Defects Original Article Series. 10*(6). New York: Liss, pp. 25-55.

Powledge, T. (1976). Can genetic screening prevent occupational disease? *New Scientist, 71*(1016), 486-488.

President's Commission on Mental Health. (1978). *Commission Report. Volumes I and II*. Washington, DC: U.S. Government Printing Office.

President's Commission for the Study of Ethical Problems in Medicine and Biomedical and Behavioral Research. (1983). *Screening and counseling for genetic conditions. A report on the ethical, social, and legal implications of genetic screening, counseling, and education programs*. Washington, DC: U.S. Government Printing Office.

Rains, P. M., Kitsuse, J. I., Duster, T., & Friedson, E. (1975). The labeling approach to deviance. In N. Hobbs (Ed.), *Issues in the classification of children: A sourcebook on categories, labels and their consequences*. San Francisco: Jossey-Bass.

Reagan warns hospitals after "Infant Doe" death. (1982, July) *Nation's Health, 8*.

Reed, S. (1974). A short history of genetic counseling. *Social Biology, 21*, 332-339.

Regensburg, J. (1978). *Toward education for health professionals*. New York: Harper & Row.

Reilly, P. (1977). *Genetics, law, and social policy*. Cambridge, MA: Harvard University Press.

Reilly, P. (1978). Government support of genetic services. *Social Biology, 25*, 23-32.
Riccardi, V. M. (1977). *The genetic approach to human disease.* New York: Oxford University Press.
Rice, N., & Doherty, R. (1982). Reflections on prenatal diagnosis: The consumers' views. *Social Work in Health Care, 1982, 8*(1), 47-57.
Robinson, J., Tennes, K., & Robinson, A. (1975). Amniocentesis: Its impact on mothers and infants—A one-year follow-up study. *Clinical Genetics, 8*, 97-106.
Roe v. Wade, 410 U.S. 113 (1973).
Schild, S. (1964). Parents of children with phenylketonuria. *Children, 11*, 92-96.
Schild, S. (1966). The challenging opportunity for social workers in genetics. *Social Work, 11*, 22-28.
Schild, S. (1968). *Parental adjustment to phenylketonuria.* Unpublished doctoral dissertation. School of Social Work, University of Southern California, Los Angeles.
Schild, S. (1972). Genetic counseling. *Encyclopedia of Social Work.* Washington, DC: National Association of Social Workers, 472-476.
Schild, S. (1973). Social worker's contribution to genetic counseling. *Social Casework, 54*, 387-392.
Schild, S. (1977a, June). *A model of social work practice for genetic counseling.* Paper presented at Fordham University, New York, Symposium on Counseling of the Developmentally Disabled and Families.
Schild, S. (1977b). Social work with genetic problems. *Health and Social Work, 2*, 58-77.
Schild, S. (1979). Psychological issues in genetic counseling of phenylketonuria. In S. Kessler (Ed.), *Genetic counseling: Psychological dimensions.* New York: Academic Press.
Schild, S. (1981). Social and psychological issues in genetic counseling. In S. R. Applewhite, Busbee, D. L., and Borgaonkar, D. H. (Eds.) *Genetic screening and counseling: A multidisciplinary perspective.* Springfield, IL: Charles C Thomas.
Schultz, A. (1966). The impact of genetic disorders. *Social Work, 11*, 29-34.
Schwartz, W. (1961). The social worker in the group. In *New Perspectives on Services to Groups.* New York: National Association of Social Workers.
Schwartz, W. (1969). Private troubles and public issues: One social work job or two? *The Social Welfare Forum.* New York: Columbia University Press, pp. 22-43.
Scotch, N., & Sorenson, J. (1977). Public education and genetic counseling in Tay-Sachs screening programs. In M. M. Kaback (Ed.), *Tay-Sachs disease: Screening and prevention.* New York: Liss.
Scott, R. B. (1970). Health care priority and sickle cell anemia. *Journal of American Medical Association, 214*, 731-734.
Sell, R. R., Roghmann, K. J., & Doherty, T. (1978). Attitudes toward abortion and prenatal diagnosis of fetal abnormalities: Implications for educational programs. *Social Biology, 25*, 288-301.
Sepe, S. J., Oakley, G. P., & Manley, A. F. (1981, November). *Genetic service delivery in the United States.* Paper presented at the American Public Health Association Annual Convention, Los Angeles, California.
Severo, R. (1980, February 3-6). The genetic barrier: Job benefit or job bias? *New York Times.*
Severo, R. (1982, June 23). 59 top U.S. companies plan genetic screening. *New York Times.*
Shore, M. F. (1975). Psychological issues in counseling the genetically handicapped. In C. Birch & P. Abrecht (Eds.), *Genetics and the quality of life.* New York: Pergamon.
Silverman, P. R. (1978). *Mutual help groups: A guide for mental health workers.* Rockville, MD: National Institute of Mental Health (Publication ADM 78-646).
Silverman, P. R. (1980). *Mutual help groups: Organization and development.* Beverly Hills, CA: Sage.
Silverman, P. R., MacKenzie, D., Pettipas, M., & Wilson, E. W. (Eds.). (1974). *Helping each other in widowhood.* New York: Health Sciences.
Simon, H. A. (1976). *Administrative behavior: A study of decision-making processes in administrative organizations* (3rd ed.). New York: Free Press.
Simoni, G., Brambati, B., Danesino, C., Rossella, F., Terzoli, G. L., Ferrari, M., & Fraccaro, M. (1983). Efficient direct chromosome analyses and enzyme determinations from chorionic villi samples in the first trimester of pregnancy. *Human Genetics, 63*, 349-357.
Simos, B. G. (1979). *A time to grieve: Loss as universal human experience.* New York: Family Service Association of America.

Slovic, P., Fischhoff, B., & Lichtenstein, S. (1976). Cognitive processes and societal risk taking. In J. S. Carroll & J. W. Payne (Eds.), *Cognition and social behavior.* Hillsdale, NJ: Lawrence Erlbaum.

Sly, W. S. (1973). What is genetic counseling. In *Contemporary genetic counseling, birth defects original article series, 9*(4). New York: Liss, pp. 5–18.

Smith, D. W. (1976). *Recognizable patterns of human malformation* (2nd ed.). Philadelphia: W. B. Saunders.

Social and psychological aspects of genetic disorders: A selected bibliography. Washington, DC: National Center for Education in Maternal and Child Health.

Smith, G. F., & Berg, J. M. (1976). *Down's anomaly.* New York: Churchill Livingston.

Solnit, A. J., & Stark, M. H. (1961). Mourning and the birth of a defective child. *Psychoanalytic Study of the Child, 16,* 523–537.

Sorenson, J. R., Swazey, J. P., & Scotch, N. A. (1981). Reproductive pasts and reproductive futures: Genetic counseling and its effectiveness. *Birth Defects Original Article Series, 17*(4). New York: Liss.

Stamatoyannopoulos, G. (1974). Problems of screening and counseling in the hemoglobinopathies. In A. G. Motulsky & J. Ebling (Eds.), *Birth Defects: Proceedings of the Fourth International Conference.* Vienna: Excerpta Medica.

Steele, M. W. (1981). Genetic screening and the public well-being. In M. D. Hiller (Ed.), *Medical ethics and the law.* Cambridge, MA: Ballinger.

Stine, G. J. (1977). *Biosocial genetics.* New York: Macmillan.

Strauss, A. L., & Glaser, B. (1975). *Chronic illness and the quality of life.* St. Louis: C.V. Mosby.

Swazey, J. P. (1971). Phenylketonuria: A case study of biomedical legislation. *Journal of Urban Law, 48,* 883–931.

Tarasoff v. Regents of the University of California, 131 Cal. Rptr. 14, 551, P.2d 334 (1976).

Thompson, J. S., & Thompson, M. W. (1980). *Genetics in medicine,* 3rd ed. Philadelphia: W.B. Saunders.

Tips, R. L., Smith, G. S., Lynch, H. T., & McNutt, C. W. (1964). The whole family concept in clinical genetics. *American Journal Diseases of Children, 107,* 67–76.

Tips, R. L., & Lynch, H. T. (1968). Genetic counseling in a team setting. *Birth Defects Original Article Series, 4*(6). New York: Liss, p. 110.

Tracy, G. S., & Gussow, Z. Self help groups: A grassroots response to a need for services. *Journal of Applied Behavioral Science,* 1976, *12,* 381–396.

Tsuang, M. T., & VanderMey, R. (1980). *Genes and the mind. Inheritance of mental illness.* New York: Oxford University Press.

Tversky, A., & Kahneman, D. (1981). The framing of decisions and the psychology of choice. *Science, 211,* 453–458.

U.S. Department Health, Education, and Welfare. (1975). *What are the facts about genetic disease?* Bethesda, MD: National Institute of General Medical Sciences, Public Health Service, National Institutes of Health, DHEW Publication No. (NIH), 75-370.

Vespa, H. (1977). Barriers to the use of genetic counseling: Economic geographic, and cultural. In W. T. Hall & C. L. Young (Eds.), *Genetic disorders: Social service interventions.* Conference sponsored by the Graduate School of Public Health, University of Pittsburgh, and the Office for Maternal and Child Health, DHHS, PHS, BCHS.

Weiss, J. O. (1976). Social work and genetic counseling. *Social Work in Health Care. 2,* 5–12.

Weiss, J. O. (1977). Social development in dwarfs. In W. T. Hall & C. L. Young (Eds.), *Genetic disorders: Social service interventions.* Conference sponsored by the Graduate School of Public Health, University of Pittsburgh, and the Office for Maternal and Child Health, DHHS, PHS, BCHS.

Weiss, J. O. (1980). Recent trends in genetic programs: Implications for social workers. In E. L. Watkins (Ed.), *Social work in a state-based system of child health care.* Proceedings of 1980 Tri-Regional Workshop, sponsored by Department of Maternal and Child Health, School of Public Health, University of North Carolina, Chapel Hill and Office of Maternal and Child Health, BCHS, DHHS, 78-88.

Weiss, J. O. (1981). Psychosocial stress in genetic disorders: A guide for social workers. *Social Work in Health Care. 6,* 17–31.

Weiss, J. O. (1983, April). *Genetic disorders and birth defects in families and society: Toward interdisciplinary understanding.* Conference sponsored by the Division of Medical Genetics and Department of Social Work, Johns Hopkins Medical Institution.

Wexler, N. (1980). Will the circle be unbroken? Sterilizing the genetically impaired. In A. Milunsky & G. Annas (Eds.), *Genetics and the law, II.* New York: Plenum Press.

White, K. L. (1973, September). Life and death in medicine. *Scientific American, 229,* 22-33.

Wilson, J. M. G., & Jungner, G. (1968). *Principles and practice of screening for disease.* Geneva: World Health Organization.

Wolfensberger, W. (1981). The extermination of handicapped people in World War II Germany. *Mental Retardation, 19,* 1-7.

Index

Abortion
  individual rights and, 137–139
  psychological response, 62,63,64–65
  religious principles and, 90
  stress related to, 90
  value conflicts in, 96–98
Adoption, 36, 108–109
Adrenoleukodystrophy, 91–92,147
Advocacy, 69, 75–76, 127
Allele, 22,28,143
Alpha-fetoprotein, 47,48
Alternative health beliefs, 103–106
Amniocentesis, see also Prenatal diagnosis
  chromosomal abnormality rates and, 24,25
  definition, 46,143
  fetoscopy and, 47
  increased use of, 118
  psychological response, 62–65,88,90,119
Anencephaly, 47
Anticipatory guidance, 68
Apert syndrome, 104–105,147
Artificial insemination, 138
Assessment, see Genetic-sound assessment
Autonomy
  confidentiality and, 134
  individual rights and, 137–138
  informed consent and, 130,132,140
Autosomal dominant inheritance, see
    Single-gene disorders
Autosomal recessive inheritance, see Single-
    gene disorders
Autosome, 22,23,24,143

Binet intelligence test, 12
Blacks, see also Sickle cell anemia
  prenatal diagnosis for, 118–119

Carriers
  definition, 32,143
  genetic screening for, 45–46,113–118
    psychosocial implications, 117–118
    sickle cell anemia, 114–116
    Tay-Sachs disease, 116–117
  psychosocial responses, 54,117–118
Cat Cry syndrome, 27

Cell division, 22–23
Chorionic villi, 143
Chorionic villous biopsy, 47–48
Chromosome analyses, 45–46
Chromosome disorders, 24–28
  definition, 24
  empiric risk figures, 27–28
  incidence, 24
  numerical abnormalities, 24–26
    Down syndrome, 24–25
    incidence, 25
    nondisjunction, 24–25
    in sex chromosomes, 25–26
    trisomy, 24–25,100
  structural defects, 26–27
    definition, 26
    deletion, 27
    incidence, 26
    inversion, 27
    translocation, 26–27,93–94
Chromosomes
  in cell division, 22–23
  definition, 22,143
  monosomic, 24,26
  numbers, 22
  trisomic, 24–25,100
Chronic grief syndrome, 51
Client
  autonomy, 130,132,134,137–138,140
  ethical responsibilities towards, 129–140
    confidentiality, 133–136
    genetic data banks and, 136
    informed consent, 130–132
    nonpaternity disclosure, 135
  financial needs, 68
  genetic-social assessment of, 79–90
    of decision making, 84–86
    elements, 81–82
    intervention strategies and, 90–91
    pedigree, 82–84
    psychosocial risk factors, 88–90
    risk-taking behavior, 84–86
  major concerns of, 7–8
  material needs, 68
  psychosocially high-risk

159